FISH OUT OF WATER

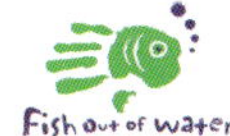

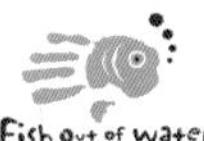
Fish out of water.

FISH OUT OF WATER

Baltimore's Fin-tastic Voyage

ORANGE FRAZER *PRESS*
Wilmington, Ohio

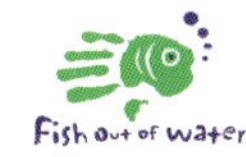

ISBN 1-882203-79-8

Published by Orange Frazer Press, Wilmington, Ohio
Photography: Patricia Venturino
James Durham
Editor: Leslie Landsman
Cover design: Tim Fauley
Printed in Canada

Library of Congress Cataloging-in-Publication Data

Fish Out of Water (Exhibition) (2001 : Baltimore, Md.)
Fish Out of Water : Baltimore's fin-tastic voyage / photography by
Patricia Venturino & James Durham.
p. cm.
ISBN 1-882203-79-8
1. Fishes in art—Exhibitions. 2. Public
sculpture—Maryland—Baltimore—Exhibitions. 3. Community art
projects—Maryland—Baltimore—Exhibitions. I. Venturino, Patricia,
1952- II. Durham, James, 1950- III. Title.
N7668.F57 F58 2001
731'.8327'0747526—dc21

2001051003

Additional copies of *Fish Out Of Water* or other Orange Frazer Press books may be ordered directly from:

Orange Frazer Press, Inc.
Box 214
37½ West Main Street
Wilmington, Ohio 45177

Telephone 1.800.852.9332 for price and shipping information
Web Site: www.orangefrazer.com

Every effort was made to correctly include and identify all fish and artists. Any omission or error is purely unintentional.

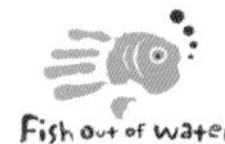

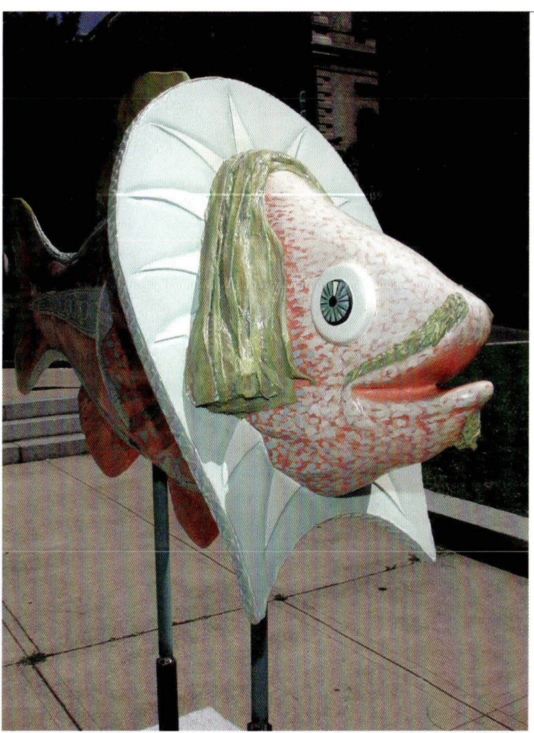

"To sea or not to sea? That is the question."
—McBass

This book is dedicated to all the people who were charmed by the school of fish swimming around the City of Baltimore.

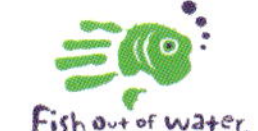

ACKNOWLEDGEMENTS

When the Cows on Parade project caught the attention of the national press and the imagination and fancy of citizens across the country, Leslie Landsman, Manager of Volunteer Services at the National Aquarium in Baltimore, immediately thought that Baltimore was a natural for a similar public art project. With Baltimore's waterfront location as the gateway to the Chesapeake Bay and its worldwide reputation for excellent seafood, it was quickly apparent that a fish was the logical choice for our City's public art display.

Leslie took her vision for the *Fish Out of Water* project to Baltimore City Councilwoman Catherine Pugh, who quickly reeled in the enthusiastic support of Baltimore Mayor Martin O'Malley. There was no turning back. Baltimore was goin' fishin'!

The first order of business was forming a working committee to organize and implement the project. Leslie and Catherine approached Michele Whelley, president of Downtown Partnership of Baltimore, to provide the organizational structure for the project. With Michele and Downtown Partnership on board, the *Fish Out of Water* Advisory Committee (FOW) was formed around a core group of "volunteers" who accepted the challenge to see the project through to completion. Seed funding from the Abell Foundation enabled the Advisory Committee to hire Mary Sue McCarthy as the project manager. It was the fall of 2000, and the goal was to launch the *Fish Out of Water* project at the opening of Baltimore's Waterfront Festival in April 2001.

The *Fish Out of Water* project found significant support from its honorary chairs William L. Jews, Richard C. "Mike" Lewin, Michele L. Whelley, Councilwoman Catherine Pugh and of course Mayor Martin O'Malley. Sue Hess, well known in Maryland State and local arts circles, lured in leading corporate citizens as our major sponsors. The Rouse Company and its CEO, Anthony W. Deering, agreed to sponsor the launch of the first fish. Phillips Seafood Restaurant, famous for serving Maryland's best seafood, threw a whale of a party to

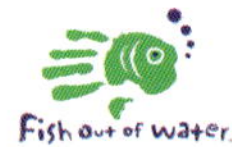

celebrate the launch. Legg Mason, Inc. and its chairman, Raymond A. "Chip" Mason, came on board to sponsor the *Legg Mason Big Catch Dinner and Auction* in November, 2001.

Other early sponsors included The Harry L. Gladding Foundation, the France-Merrick Foundation, the Baltimore Area Convention and Visitors Association, the Maryland Department of Business and Economic Development, The Whiting Turner Contracting Company, A & R Development corporation, and the National Aquarium in Baltimore.

The law firm of Venable, Baetjer and Howard, LLP provided legal services pro bono to insure the integrity of the project for all involved. Loretta Layman from Venable provided hours of administrative support for all aspects of the project. The Maryland Institute of Art offered to provide warehouse space for all the fish. The City of Baltimore agreed to help with the installation of the fish. MGH Advertising created the *Fish Out of Water* logo.

It would take an encyclopedia to adequately acknowledge and thank everyone who supported and worked to make *Fish Out of Water* the astonishing success it is. But we are going to give it a shot!

First and foremost, we applaud Leslie Landsman who has been the project's Creative Director and keeper of the integrity of the project as public art. And without Councilwoman Catherine Pugh we would never have achieved the level of corporate, philanthropic, and personal financial support that was needed to sponsor 180 incredibly imaginative and fanciful fish.

Our Project Manager, Mary Sue McCarthy, worked tirelessly to keep us on track, and Lynne Nemeth, whom we hired to organize the live and Internet auctions, helped us focus on these two events. Sue Hess put her energy into chairing the auction. Suzi and Dave Cordish were gracious hosts of our preview party. Scott Robertson from Engine Performance also provided invaluable help. We also want to acknowledge all the members of this Advisory Committee: Karen Bokram, Neal Borden, Sita Culman, Joan Davidson, Newt Fowler, Bill Gilmore, Sue Hess, Gary Kachadourian, Leslie Landsman, Fred Lazarus, Tia Malloy, Jack Rasmussen, Paul Rome, Clair Segal, Denise Velgouse and Michele Whelley.

The individuals involved in producing, selecting and installing the art provided Baltimore residents and visitors months of excitement and discovery over the summer and fall of 2001. Steven Weitzman

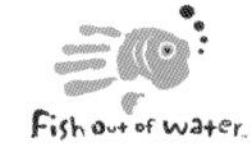

of Weitzman Studios, Inc. created the sculpture that became our special species of fish, *Ichthyaerius Baltimoris*, (commonly known as "aerial fish from Baltimore") and fabricated 200 fish without a hitch. The artistic review committee selected approximately 230 designs from the over 500 designs proposed by local and regional artists. Members of the committee include Jack Rasmussen, Clair Segal, Dr. Leslie King-Hammond, Jennifer Fleming, Bill Gilmore, Mary Ann Mears, Carla Dunlop, and Gary Kachadourian. Ken Tomlinson from Everlasting Vault Company manufactured the 700 pound bases to support the fish with engineering help from Tim Sibol of Skarda and Associates. Paul Scurti and his crew of City Public Works employees installed the bases and moved the fish all around Baltimore. Civic Works and Scott Saxman provided the manpower to install the art on the bases. Amanda Hogan produced our fish plaques.

More help was still needed. The business advisory committee culled through lists and lists of area corporations and each person had the assignment of hooking as many of the corporations as possible to sponsor a fish. These individuals are Neal Borden, Sita Culman, Mike Lewin, Lenny Kaplan, Gail Kaplan, Tracy Gosson, Catherine Pugh, Mary Sue McCarthy, Michele Whelley, Larry La Motte, Adrian Harpool, Sue Hess, Nancy Haragan, Janet Marie Smith, Paul Wolman, and Newt Fowler. When we were ready to launch our web site, Paul Manion provided designs and Marc Frazcati provided the technical expertise and manpower to maintain our website, www.baltimorefish.org.

Public relations, marketing, and event expertise were provided by Richard Cross, Heidi Griebel, Jay McCutcheon, Nicole M^c^Glynn, Meghann Siwinski, Jay Frankland and Rupi Virdee, all Downtown Partnership staff; Paula Rome, Joan Davidson, Nancy Hinds, Roz Healy, Sheila Goodwin, Tracey Baskerville; and MGH Advertising. Joan Davidson, oversaw the creation of retail product with the help of Cindy Schmidt from Maryland Screen Printers and Colleen McKenna from the Collateral Group. Mary Pat Andrea, Michael Durham, Neil Adelman, and Paula Rome rounded out the committee.

The challenge of locating all of the fish once they were installed was addressed by *The Baltimore Sun,* which printed the first map, followed by Georganne Commarata, the extraordinarily talented designer from the Baltimore Area Convention and Visitors Association, who designed the final O-Fish-al Finder map. Chesapeake Advertising, Inc. donated the printing of the map. The advertising firm of

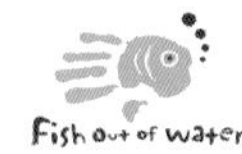

Trahan, Burden and Charles contributed their incredibly talented staff to design the invitation to the Auction and the Auction Catalog.

The list is endless: The Annie E. Casey Foundation and Anheuser Busch who sponsored many of the community fish, as well as those community organizations that collaborated on sponsoring their fish; the Executive Director of the National Aquarium in Baltimore, David Pittenger and his staff for their support; more than 250 corporations, organizations and institutions that either sponsored Fish or incorporated *Fish Out Of Water* into their own events and celebrations. And we thank countless others who embraced this project.

Proceeds from the *Fish Out of Water* auctions and the sales of retail products, including this book, will go to City youth and arts programs. These programs include: Be-Instrumental Fine Arts Education in Baltimore City Public Schools; Arts Education Programs funded through (MACAC) the Mayor's Advisory Committee on Art and Culture (MACAC) CityArts Grants; and the Mayor's initiative to wire the classrooms. We believe that the additional legacy of this project can be a greater appreciation of public art and a realization that art can enrich our lives.

Fish Out of Water
Advisory Committee

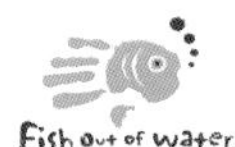

TABLE OF CONTENTS

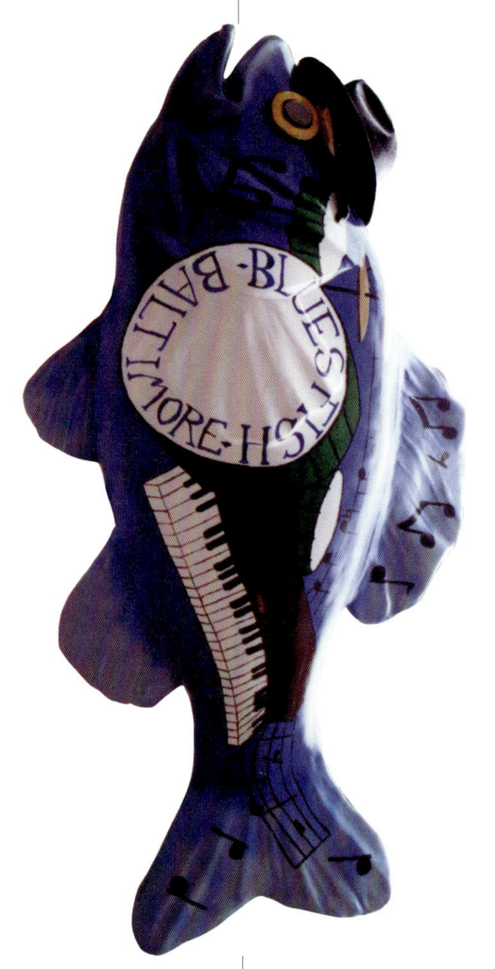

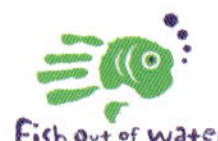

FOREWORD

IN THE YEAR 2001, EXTRAORDINARY THINGS HAPPENED IN BALTIMORE. The Ravens won the Super Bowl and the city was awash in purple and black. Cal Ripken, the iron man of baseball, announced his retirement from the Baltimore Orioles and fans flooded Camden Yards at Oriole Park. A new wild and wonderful, brilliantly diverse fish species arrived in Baltimore-*Ichthyaerius Baltimoris* —commonly known as the "aerial fish from Baltimore"—and The Fish Out of Water urban art project was born.

These fin-tastic fish are big fish: six feet long and three feet high and have the most infectious smiles on their lips. They have the ability to cause people to giggle and to make children and adults bubble up with delight. They carry briefcases, they wear hats, they are covered with feathers and formstone, they carry frogs on their backs, they are hairy, they play music, and they glow in the dark—and all of that is just for starters.

More than 150 local and regional artists brought these fish to life and the public was hooked by their charm. Sponsors from all parts of the Baltimore community were lured in to provide funds for the creation of this school of fish. People from everywhere explored the streets of the City in search of each and every fish. Each one is an eye-catching surprise. The fish provided a common denominator of fun that everyone talked about, and a true spirit of community erupted in the City. People from all neighborhoods and every walk of life found ways to enjoy this public art exhibit.

The City was caught in a wave of fish fever. Tourists visited the city with cameras, plenty of film, and money to spend in local restaurants and hotels. Groups took fish tours throughout the city. Fish appeared on television, and in newspapers and magazines. Radio stations had all sorts of fish tales to catch the attention of their listeners.

The fish have charmed Charm City. Their presence has brought life to the City and unexpected pleasure to thousands.

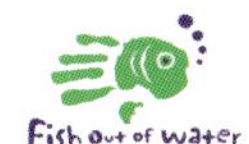

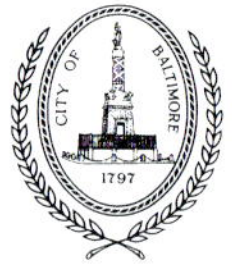

MARTIN O'MALLEY
Mayor
250 City Hall
Baltimore, Maryland 21202

Greetings from Baltimore, the habitat of the most elegant and whimsical creatures ever seen.

Those of you who visited Baltimore during the last few months know what I'm talking about. The *Fish Out of Water* public art project brought more than 160 funky fish sculptures to the streets of Baltimore. With names like *State Grouper*, *Fish Out of John Waters*, *Cast Iron Cal*, and *Shark Lark*, these colorful creations brought charm and excitement to our city, showcased the tremendous talent of some local artists, and ultimately helped us raise funds for a trio of youth arts programs.

This book is the definitive record of the fish that swam around Baltimore during the summer and fall of 2001. As you flip through these colorful pages, many of you who had the chance to see the fish in person will become hooked on this project all over again, while those of you who did not will get a sense of what all the excitement was all about.

A lot of time, creativity, and hard work on the part of hundreds of people went into making this project a success. While space does not permit me to acknowledge by name everyone who was responsible, I'd like to pay special thanks to Councilwoman Catherine Pugh and *Fish Out of Water* creative director Leslie Landsman. Without their efforts, this project would have been dead in the water.

This is a very auspicious – or should I say "aus-fish-cious" – time in Baltimore's history. I hope you like what you see in this book. Most importantly, I hope you will visit Baltimore soon in order to experience the many other charms that only the "Greatest City in America" can offer.

Sincerely,

Mayor

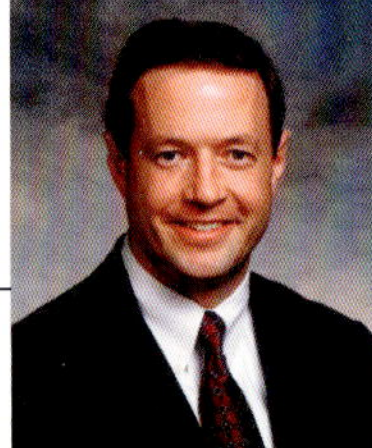

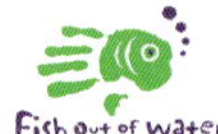

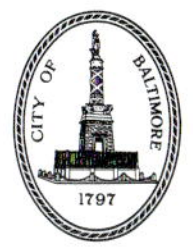

BALTIMORE CITY COUNCIL

CATHERINE E.
PUGH
Fourth District

CHAIRPERSON:
LABOR AND ECONOMIC
DEVELOPMENT SUBCOMMITTEE

VICE CHAIRPERSON:
URBAN AND INTER-
GOVERNMENTAL
AFFAIRS COMMITTEE

MEMBER:
FINANCE COMMITTEE

LAND USE AND PLANNING
COMMITTEE

When I approached Mayor Martin O'Malley with the idea of doing the *Fish Out of Water* public art exhibit in the fall of 1999, he smiled and said, "Catherine, let's go fishing."

Since then, *Ichthyaerius Baltimoris,* or "aerial fish from Baltimore," has been a wonderful temporary addition to Baltimore's landscape. However, it has left a permanent impression on the hearts of residents and visitors to our city.

The *Fish Out of Water* project has been a truly fin-tastic experience. Not only did we succeed in installing a "critical bass" of fish all over Downtown Baltimore, we reserved nearly two dozen fish for special placement in City neighborhoods – a first, I am told, for a public arts project of this nature.

I'm indebted to so many people for making *Fish Out of Water* a reality. First and foremost, Leslie Landsman who came to me with the idea and said can we make this happen. She volunteered countless hours of her time towards its success. She has truly been the "cod mother" of this project.

The staff of Downtown Partnership of Baltimore, along with its president, Michele Whelley, also dedicated tremendous effort and energy, as did project manager Mary Sue McCarthy and the members of *Fish Out of Water* Advisory Committee.

A special thanks to the many individual fish sponsors which included corporations, foundations, and neighborhoods. Similarly, I'd like to thank the artists – who submitted some 500 designs and created more than 180 fish.

As you leaf through the pages of this book, I hope you enjoy viewing these fish as much as I enjoyed being a part of this project.

Sincerely,

Councilwoman Catherine E. Pugh
4th District

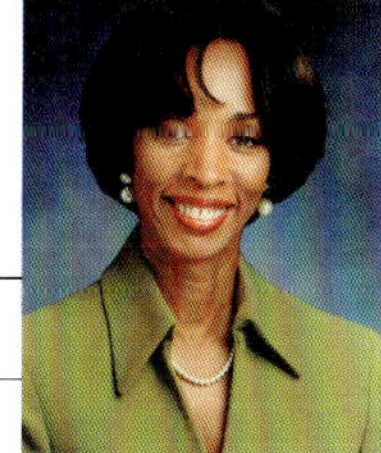

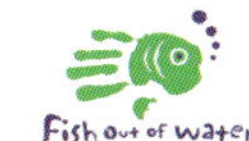

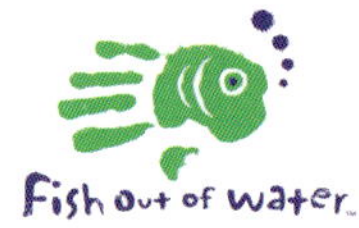

In the summer of 1999 when I saw the Cows on Parade in Chicago, I immediately thought the City of Baltimore should create its own public art exhibit. Cows seemed out of place in Baltimore, but fish seemed to be the perfect match. It was not easy convincing everyone that placing big fish all around our charming city was a good idea, but once Councilwoman Catherine Pugh threw her support behind the idea, I knew it would be come a reality.

Creating a school of fish to adorn our city streets has been both extremely challenging and remarkably rewarding. The logistics involved in creating, delivering, selling, installing, caring for, and auctioning 180 fish is enough to boggle the minds of the best of us. Somehow, with the help of many hard-working people, we succeeded. Through tears and laughter, these fish came to life and brought life to the City.

Everyone—young, old, black, white, on foot, in wheelchairs, on bicycles or buses—found a way to share the spirit and joy of the *Fish Out of Water* project. Artists learned from each other and shared tall fish tales. Sponsors took pride in ownership and communities came together to bring a fish to their own neighborhoods.

The fish have served their purpose. They have taught us how art can enrich our lives—whether it is in a museum or on the streets. They provided exposure for many talented and creative artists. They helped us raise money for city youth programs. Most of all, they gave us a reason to smile.

I am grateful to the staff and volunteers of the National Aquarium in Baltimore for allowing me take time away from the fish in the water to help create *Fish Out of Water*. I thank every single person who worked tirelessly to realize this dream and I thank the citizens of the City of Baltimore who embraced this project with great joy.

Leslie Landsman
Creative Director
Fish Out of Water

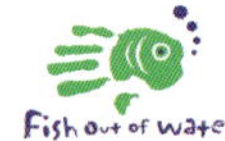

FISH OUT OF WATER

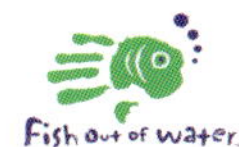

Evolution Of a Baltimore Fish Jockey

Racing to the Finish

Giddy Up fish honors the Maryland racing tradition in an aquatic parody. The multitude of racing fans in Baltimore make it an important part of the city's past and present. Who else could better jockey a fish than a frog? The blanket is a giant lily pad; the reins are seaweed and shells. The scales of the fish glitter with metallic paint highlights.

1

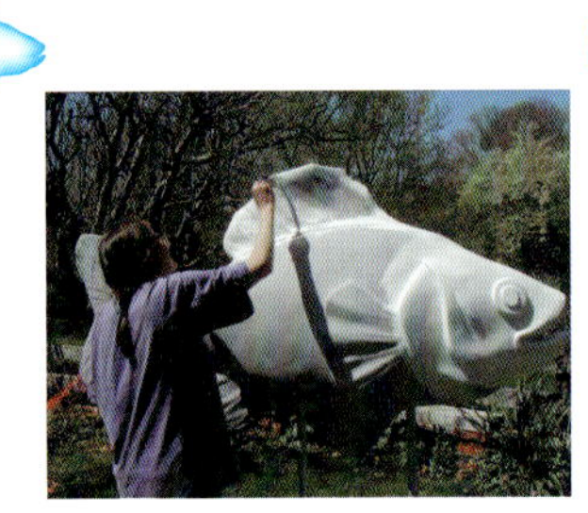

2

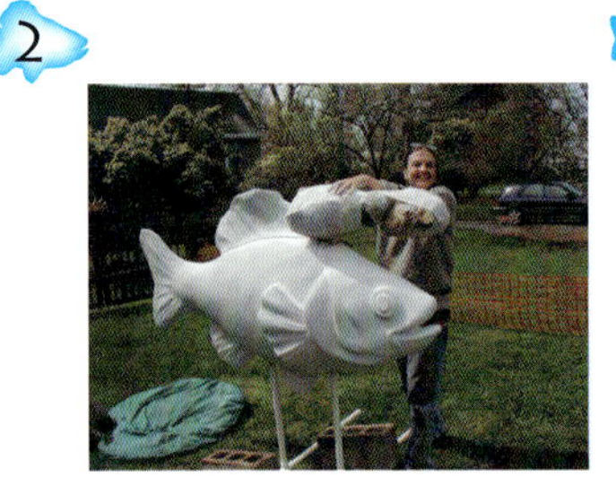

3

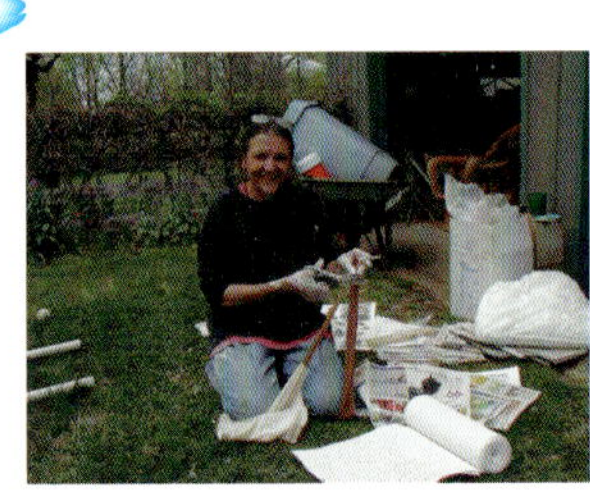

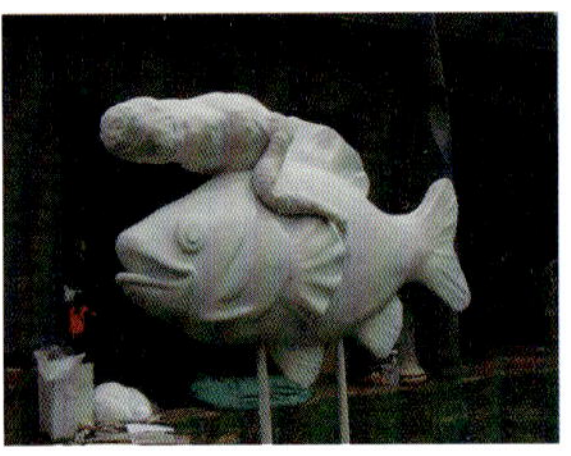

5

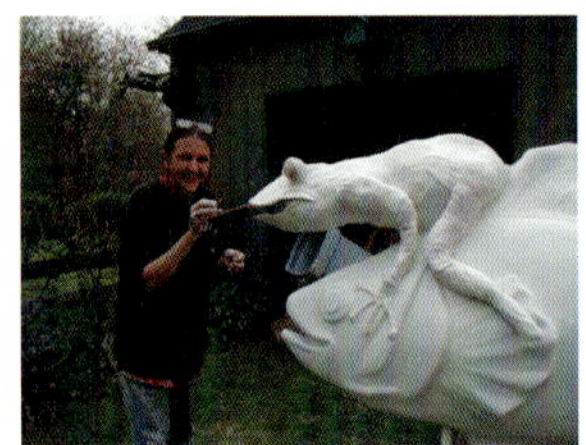

6

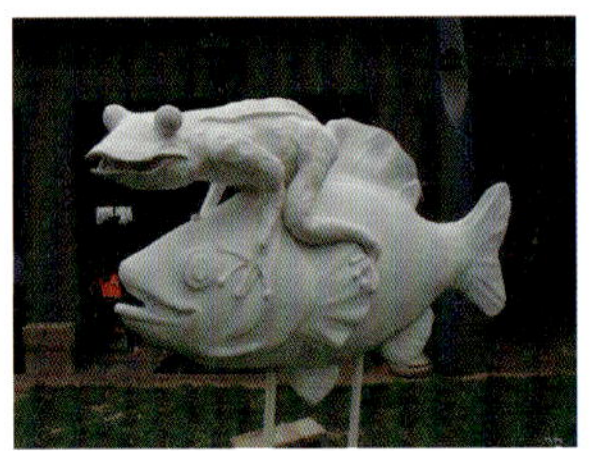

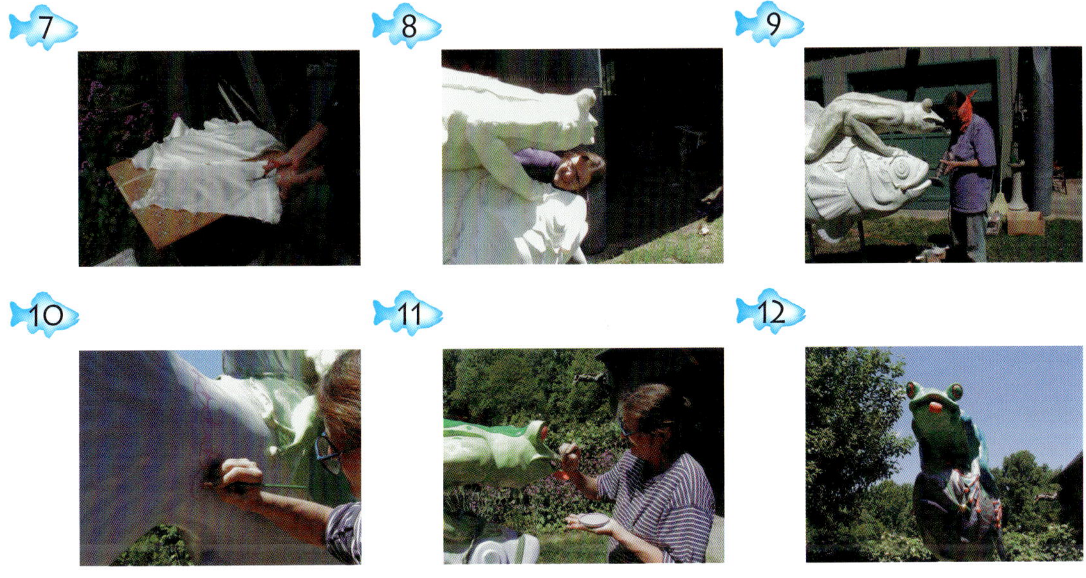

Artists Christina Davidson and Wendi Wobbe building ***Giddy Up***.

Photos by Christina Davidson

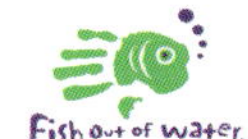

FISH WITH PASSION

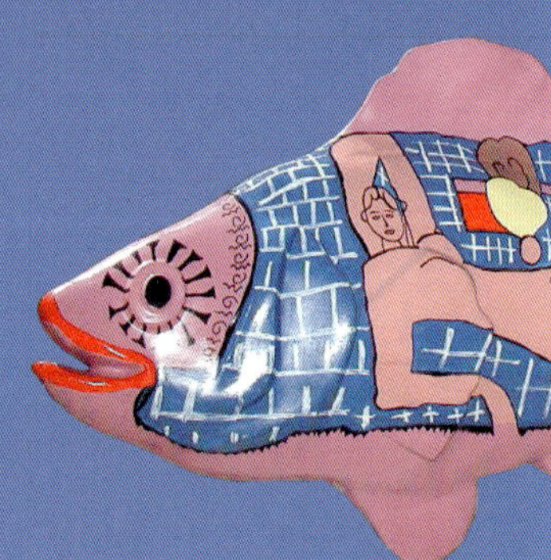

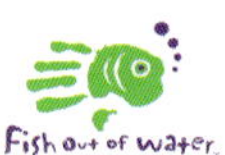

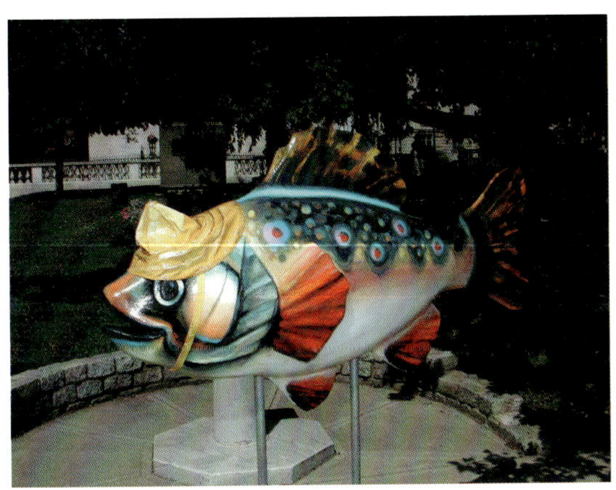

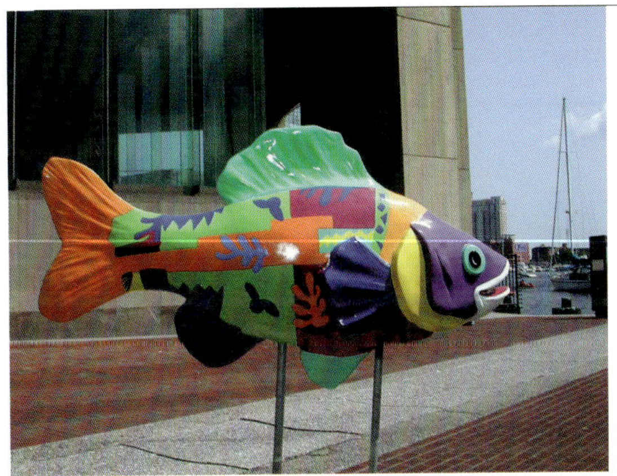

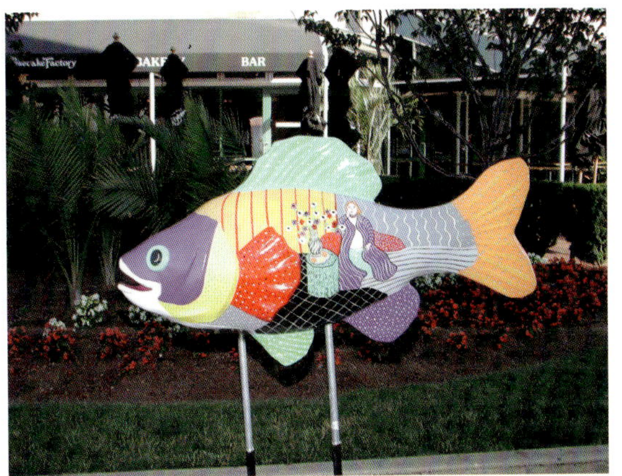

Clockwise, from top left:

WINSLOW HUMOR
Valerie Watson
France-Merrick Foundation

CONE FISH (RIGHT)
Kristin Helberg
Credit Suisse First Boston

CONE FISH (LEFT)
Kristin Helberg
Credit Suisse First Boston

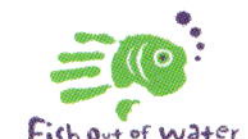

FISHCASSO
Robert Taylor
Baltimore Magazine

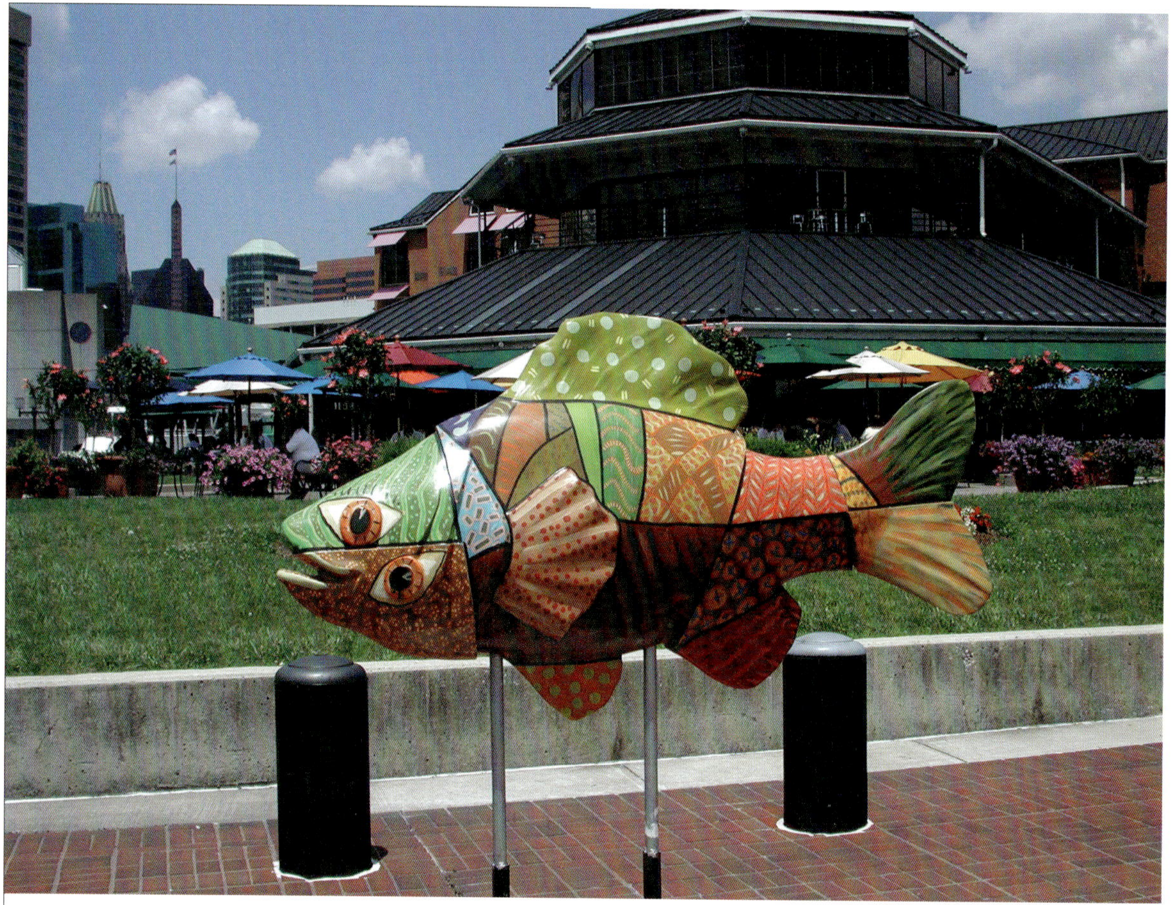

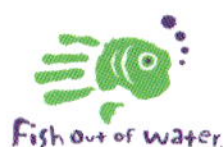

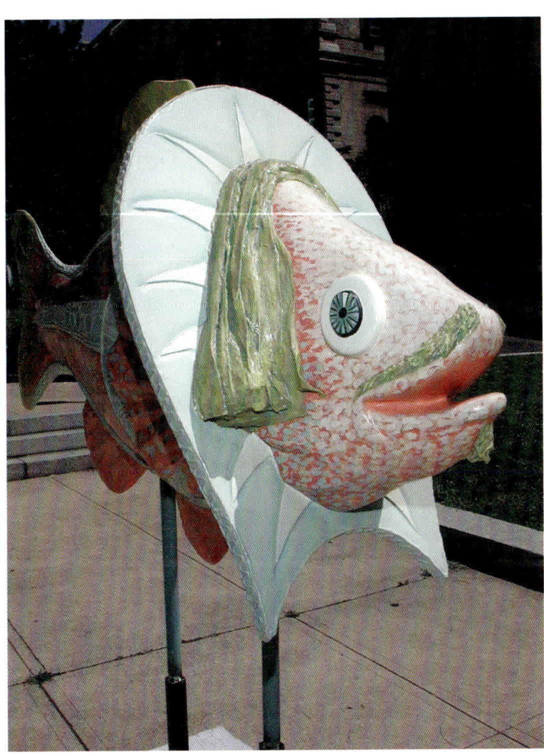

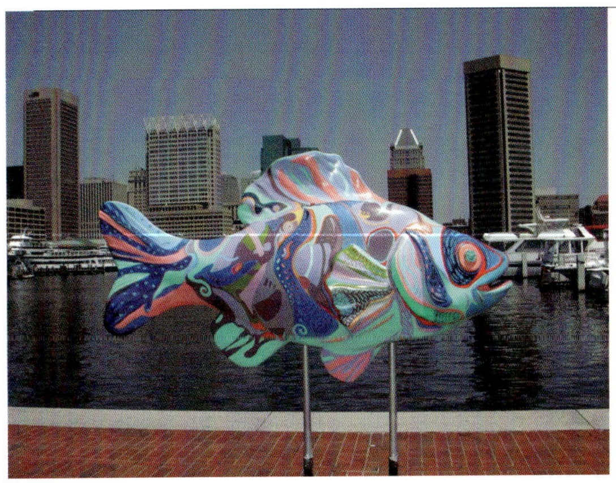

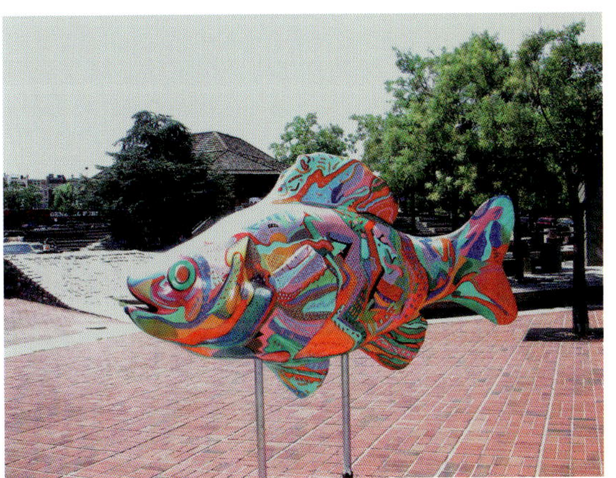

Clockwise, from top left:

WILLIAM SHAKESPERCH
Craig Brown
Center Stage

AFRICAN OPUS (RIGHT)
Greg Fletcher
Municipal Arts Society of Baltimore City

AFRICAN OPUS (LEFT)
Greg Fletcher
Municipal Arts Society of Baltimore City

Clockwise, from top left:

SWORD IN THE STONE
Clyde C. Gillam
Wilmer, Cutler & Pickering

FLOUNDERING POE
Joann Larrimore
The Time Group

STILL LIFE FISH
Phyllis Saroff
Maryland Food Bank, Courtesy of
T. Rowe Price Associates Foundation

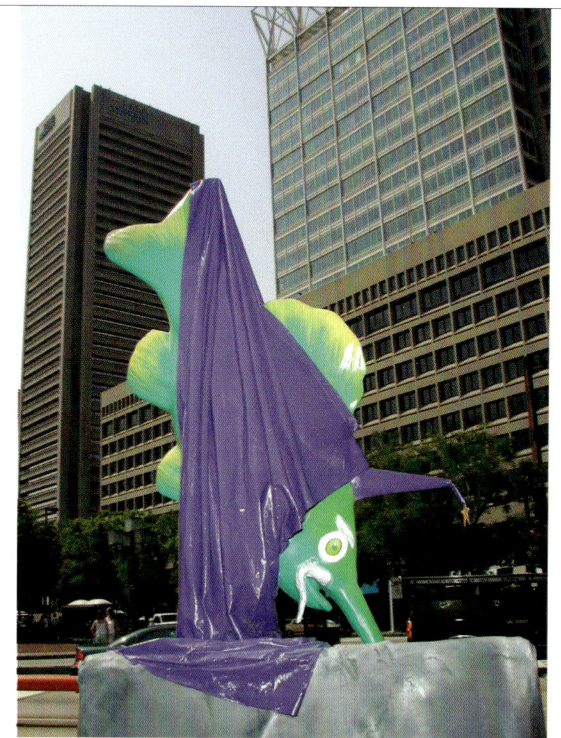

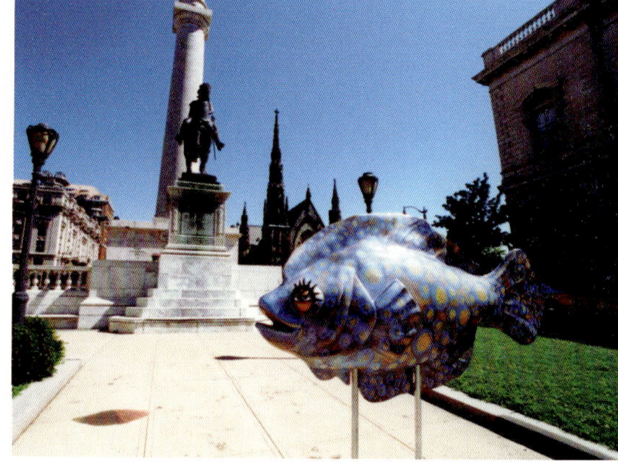

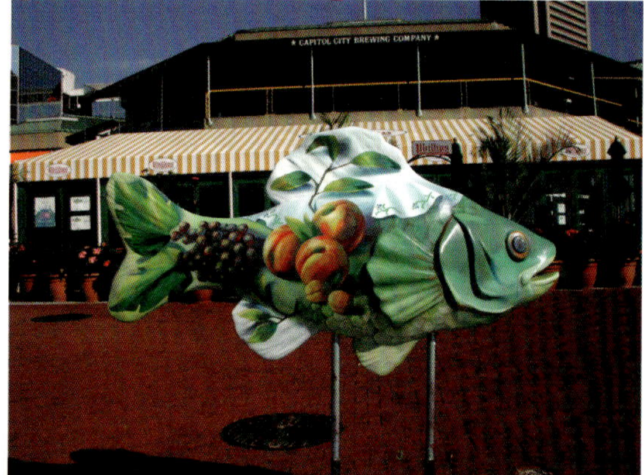

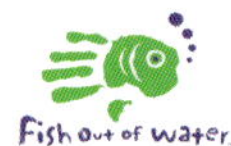

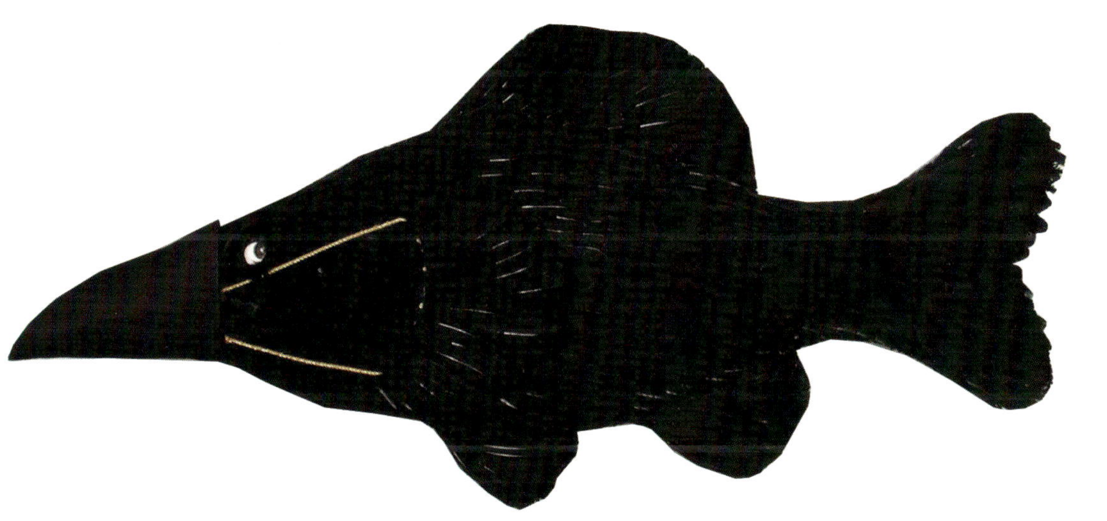

RAVEN FISH: NEVER MORE
Manon Cleary & F. Steven Kijek
URS Corporation

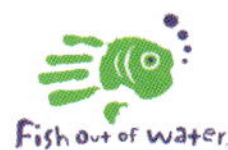

Clockwise, from top left:

PESCE DI VETRO
Anthony Corradetti
Brown Investment Advisory &
Trust Company

ART AFISHIANADO
Susan Fernandez-Janczak
Jean and Sid Silber

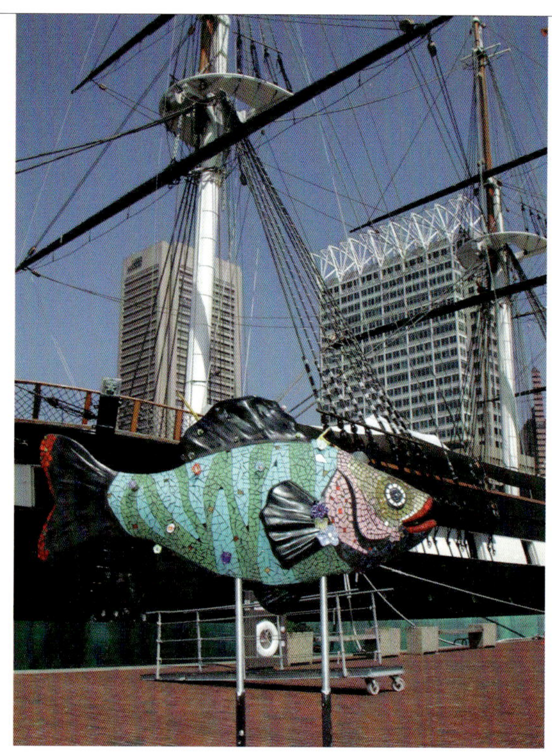

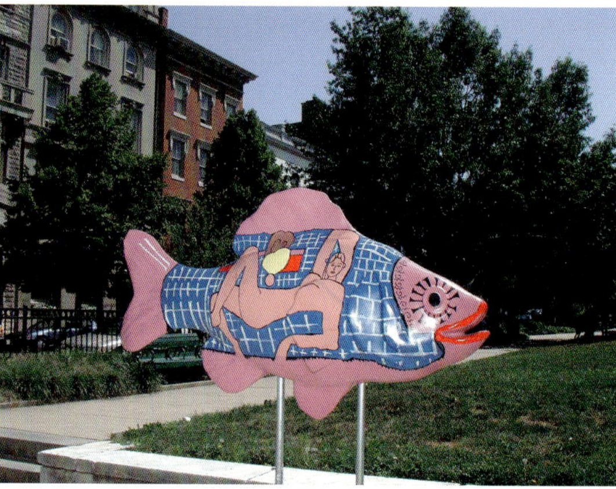

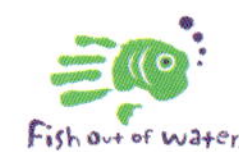

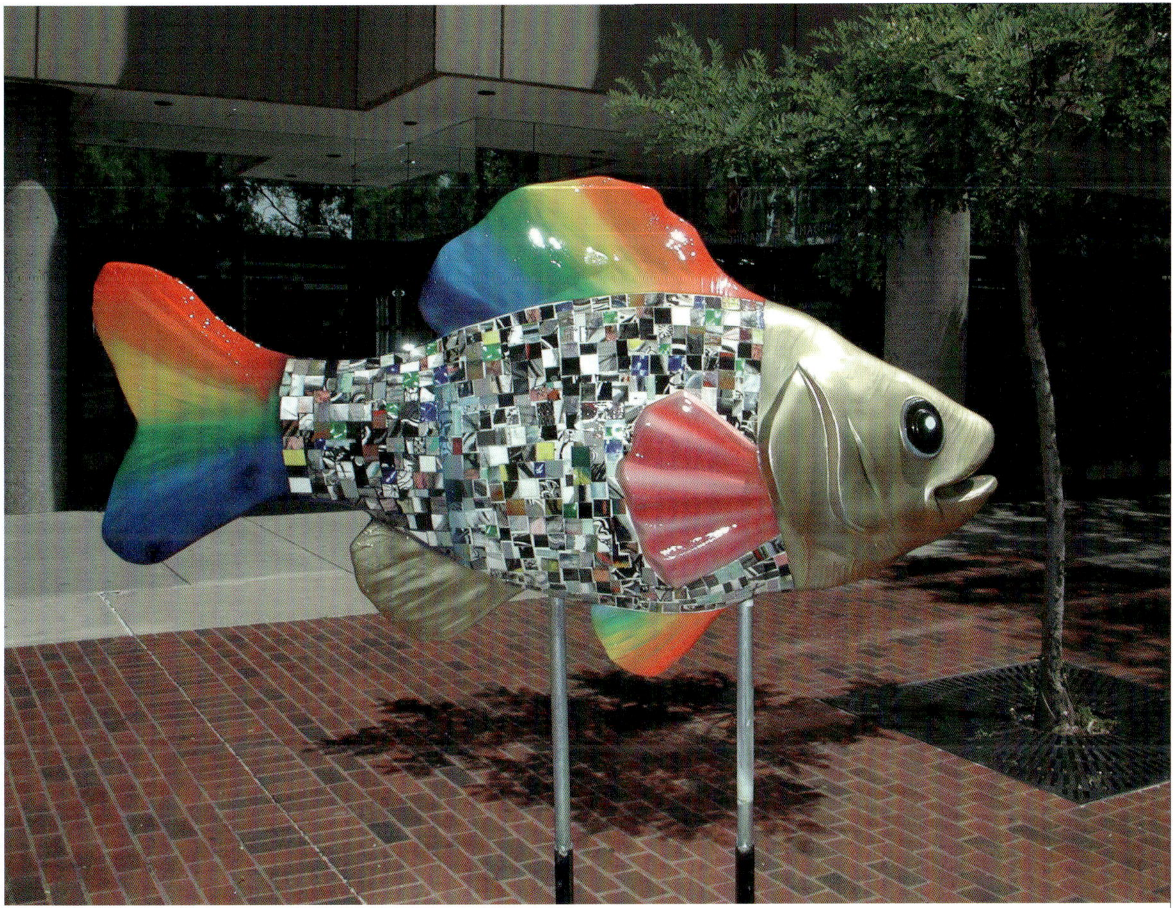

RAINBOW FISH

Rex Stevens

Pell Rudman Trust Company

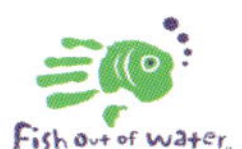

Top left:

ITALIAN FISH
Gina Pierleoni
Hord Coplan and Macht, Inc.
and Regional Management

Top right:

PERCHED, AND SAT, AND NOTHING MORE
John Aaron
Mid-Atlantic Realty Trust

Bottom left and right:

GARDEN VARIETY FISH
Gail Gorlitzz
Hyatt Regency Baltimore

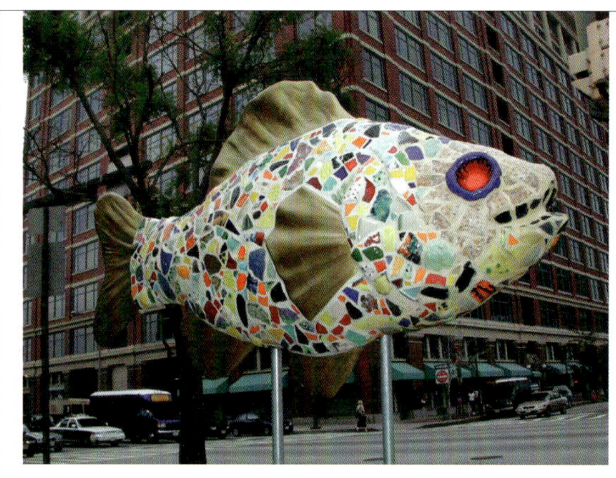

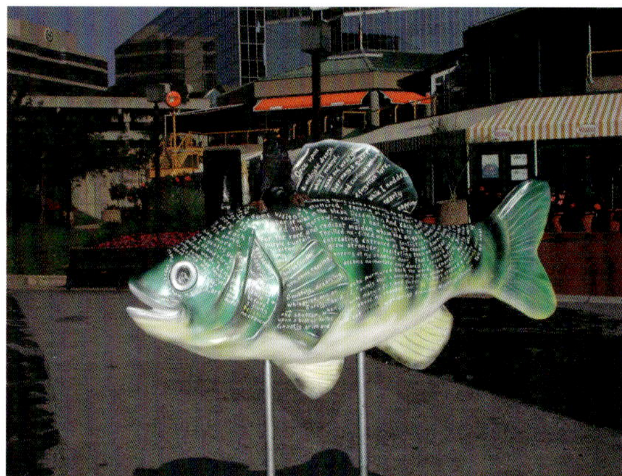

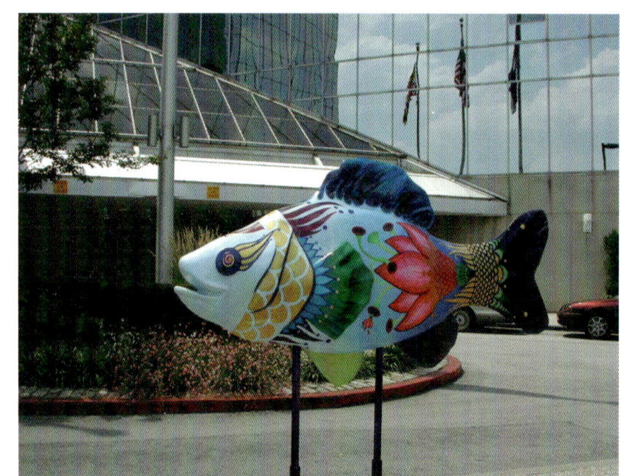

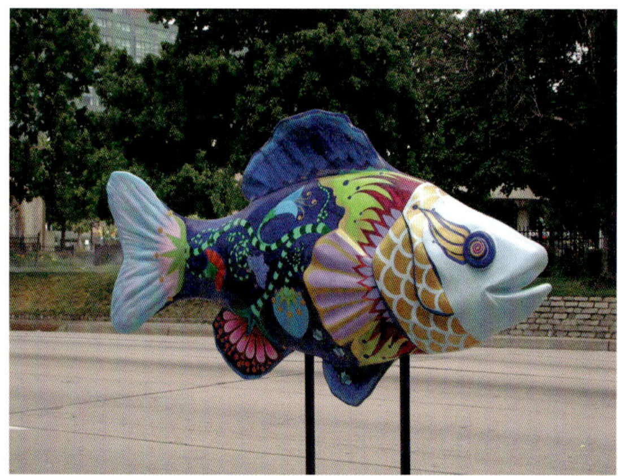

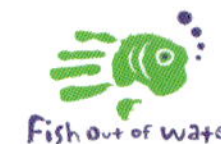

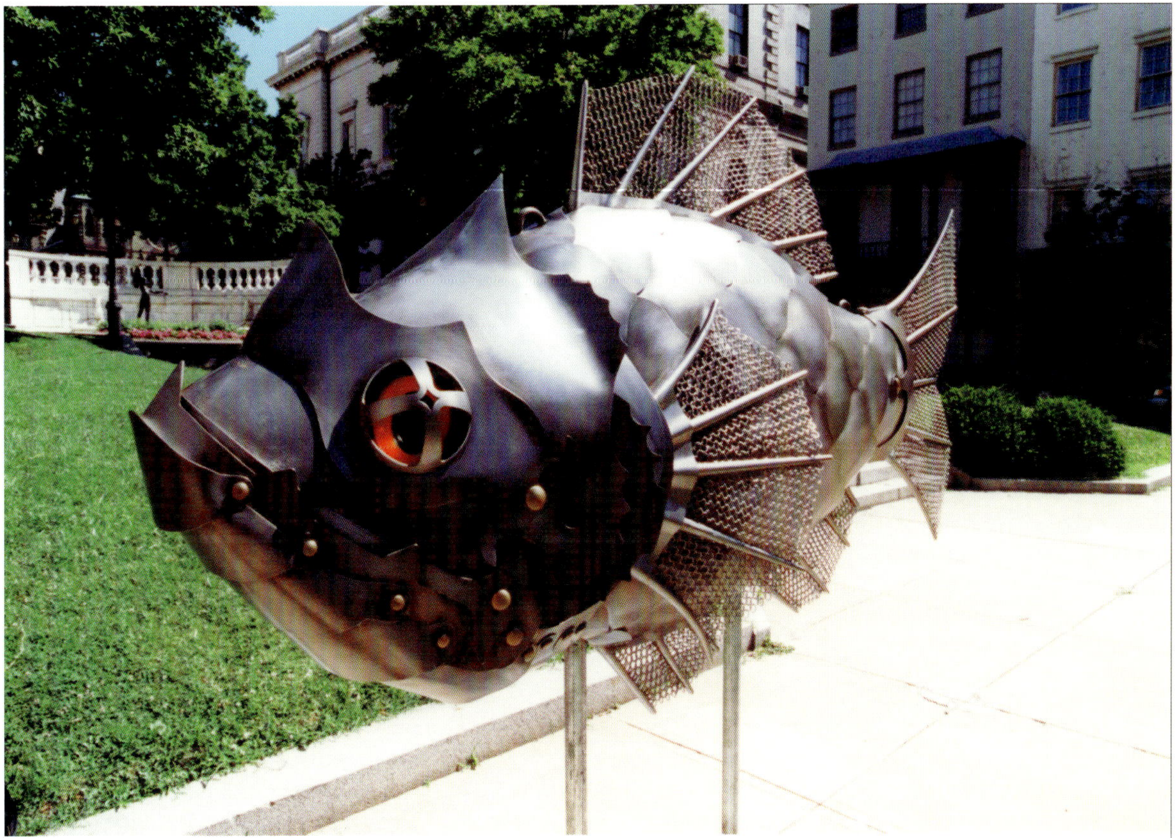

ARMORED FISH

Karl Saar

The Walters Art Museum with support from Pepsi-Cola

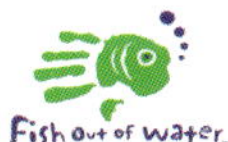

ROCK FISH—STRIPED BASS
Bonnie Printz
France-Merrick Foundation

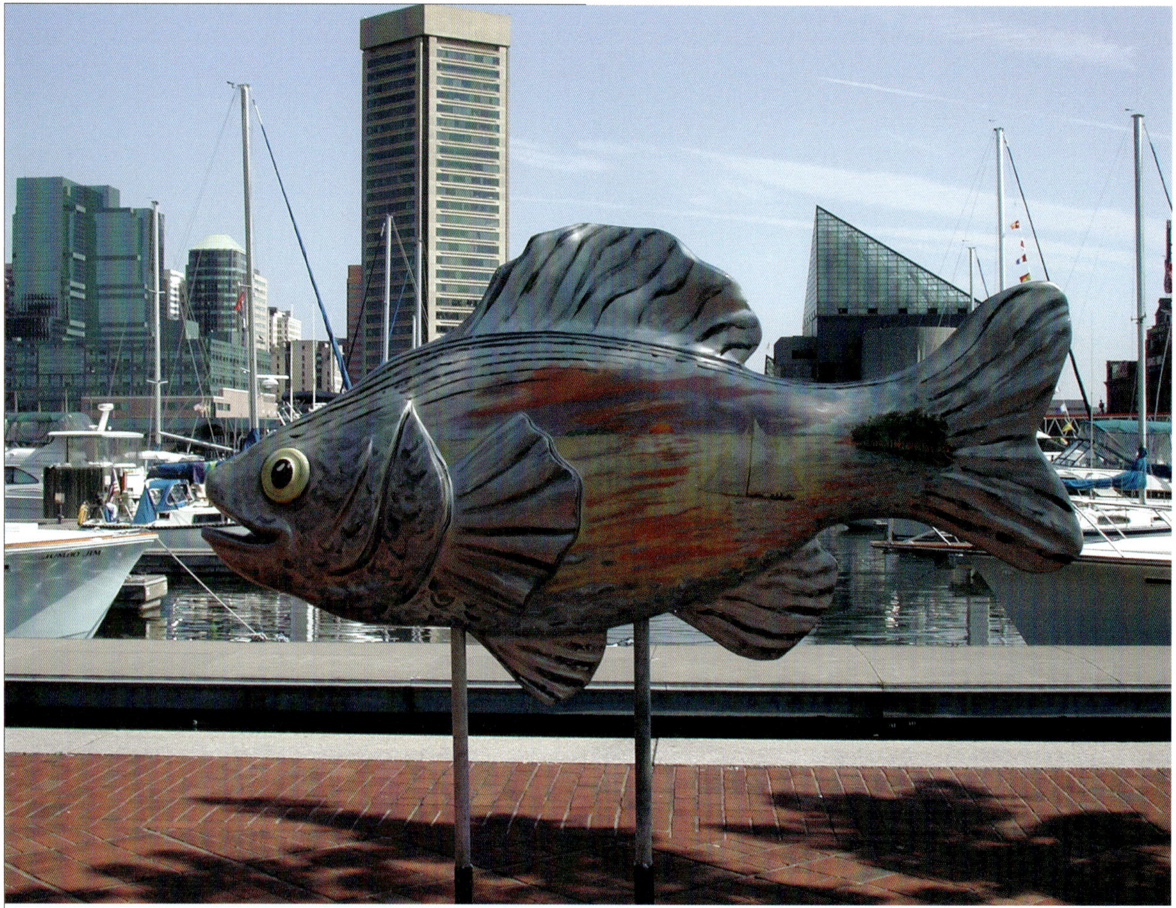

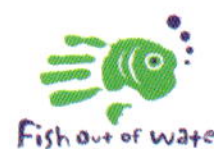

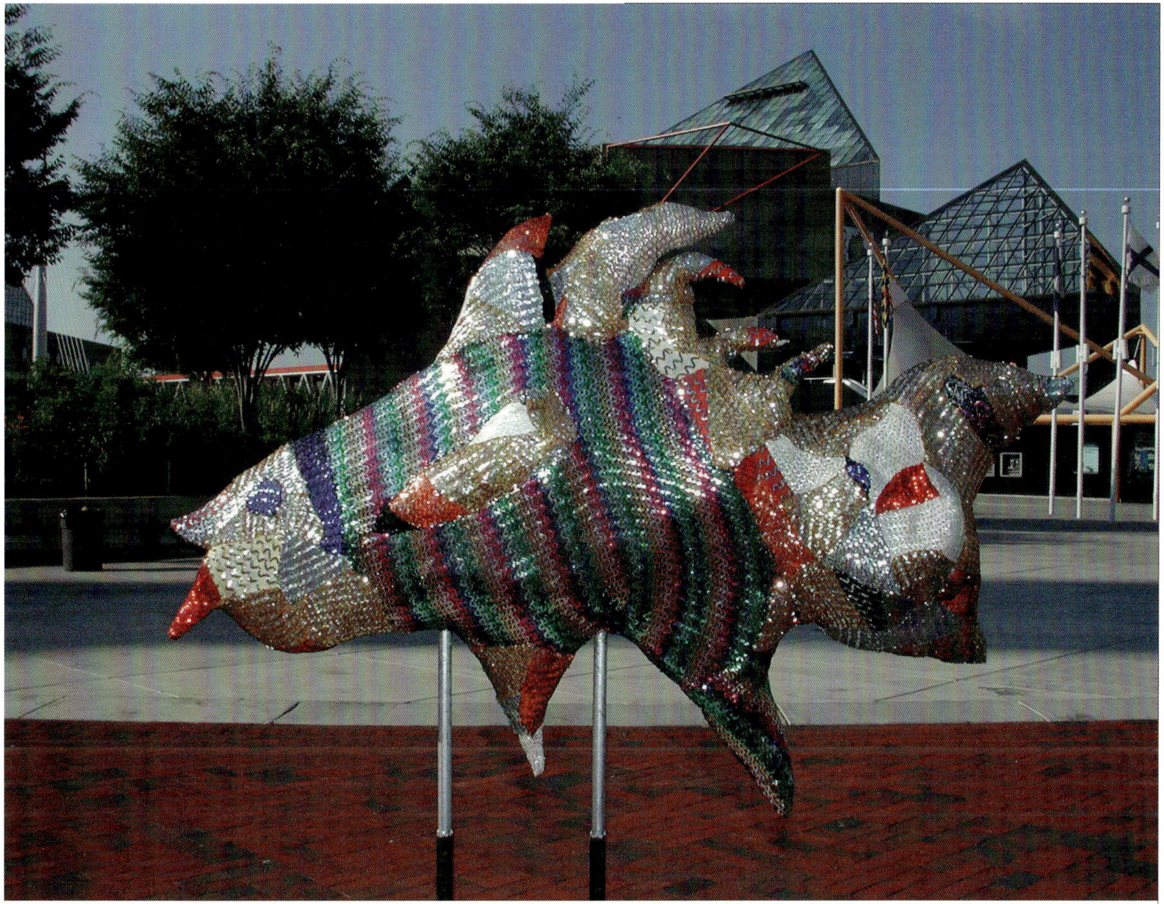

BEADED FISH
Claes Gabriel
Don Petitt,
The Sterling Group, Inc. NY, NY

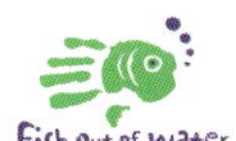

FISH ON THEIR WAY UP

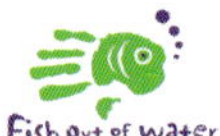

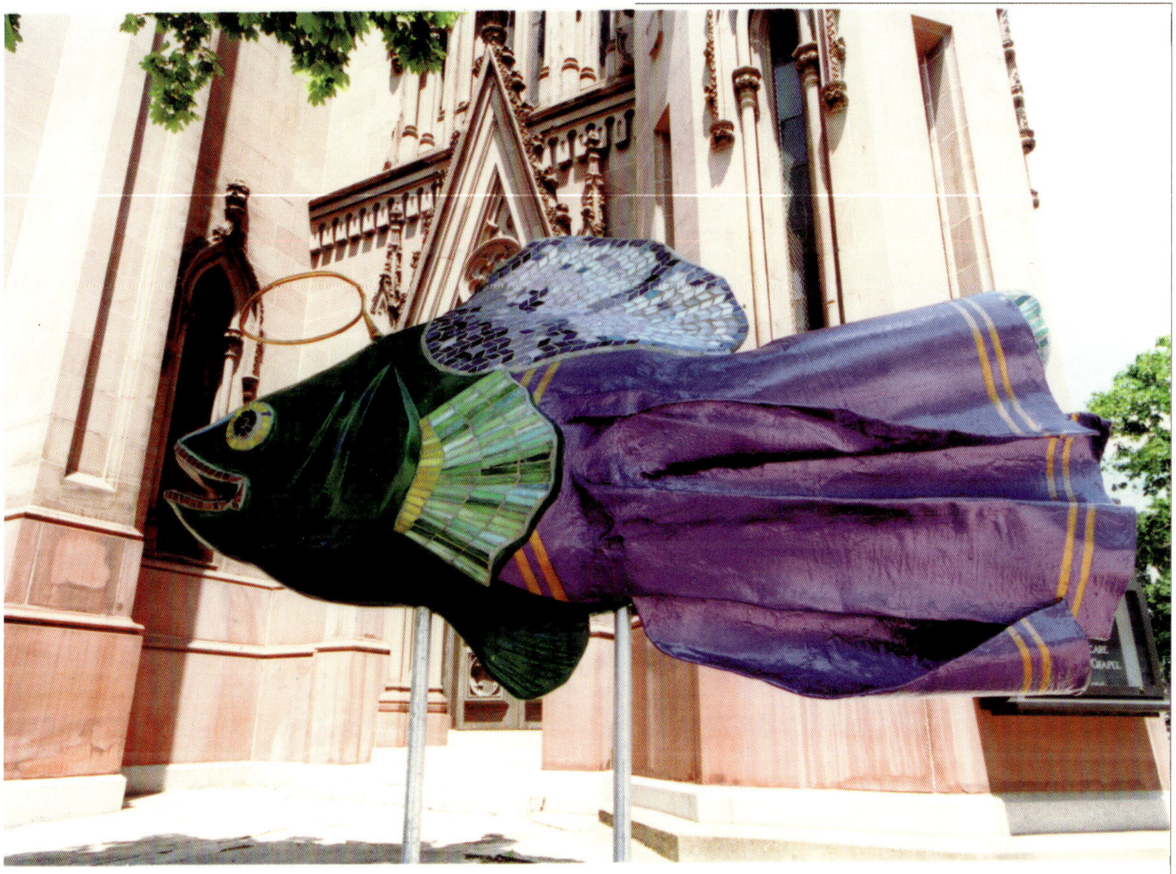

ANGEL FISH

Betty Schroll

The First and Franklin Street Presbyterian Church

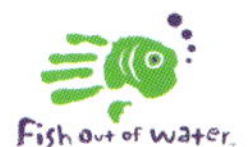

Left:

STARFISH
Melissa Daman
Friends of Annmarie Garden

Right:

STAR FISH
Lisa Manheim
Constellation Energy Group

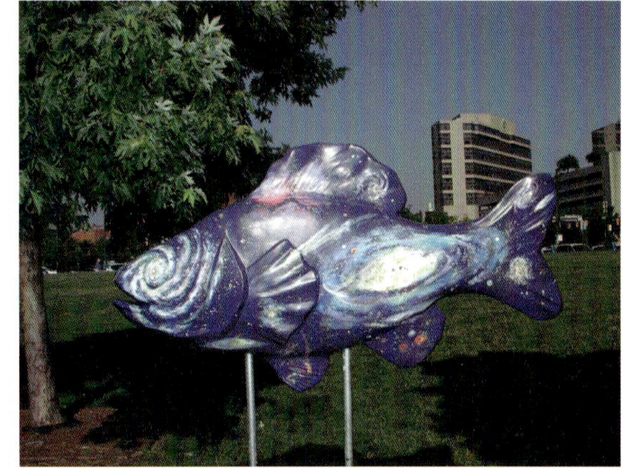

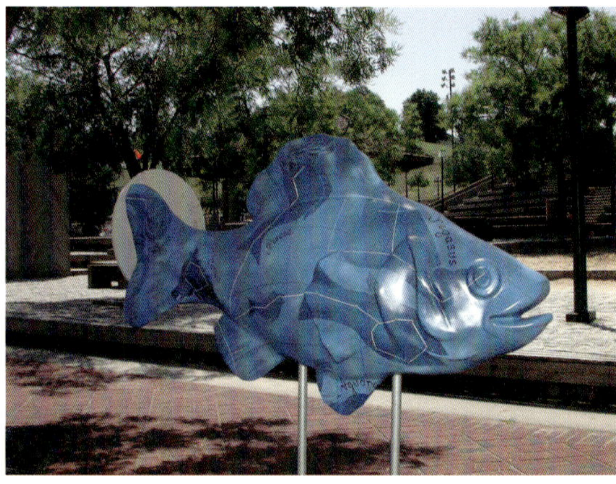

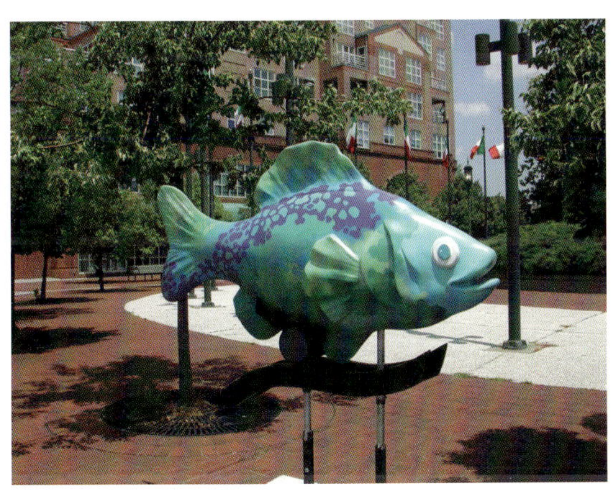

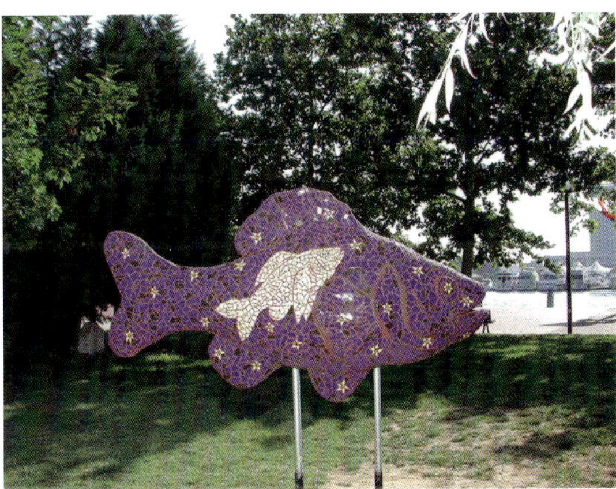

Left:

UP AND COMING FISH
Ginger Peloquin
MERRITT Properties, LLC

Right:

CELESTIAL
Mae Lucier
Tide Point Day Care/
Board of Childcare

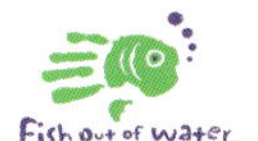

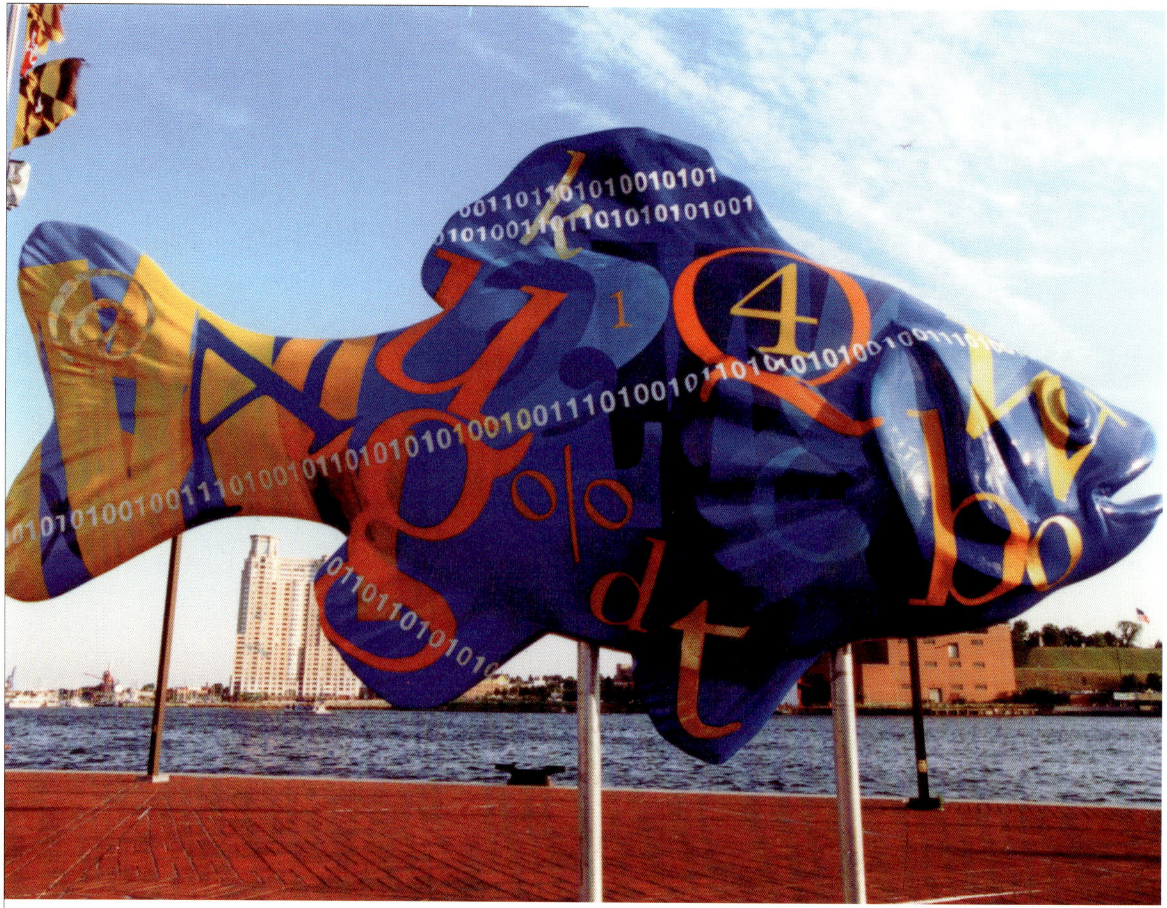

A FISH WITH CHARACTER
Amanda Joy Gingery/
Villa Julie College
Grant Thornton, LLP

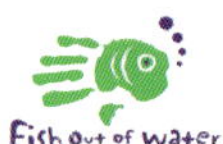

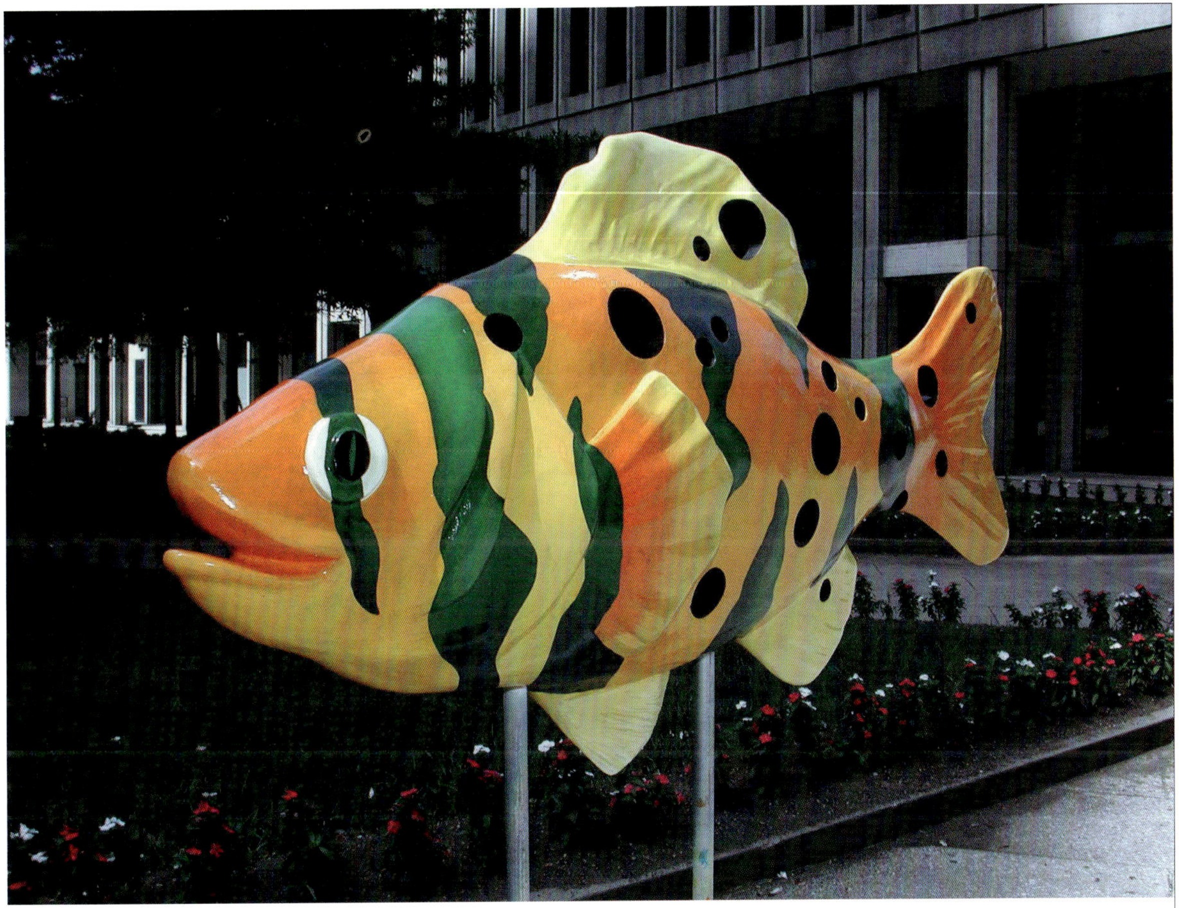

HOLY MACKERAL
Michael W. Anthony and Sarah Barnes
Gallagher, Evelius & Jones LLP

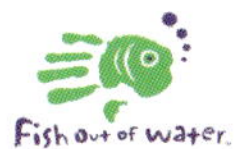

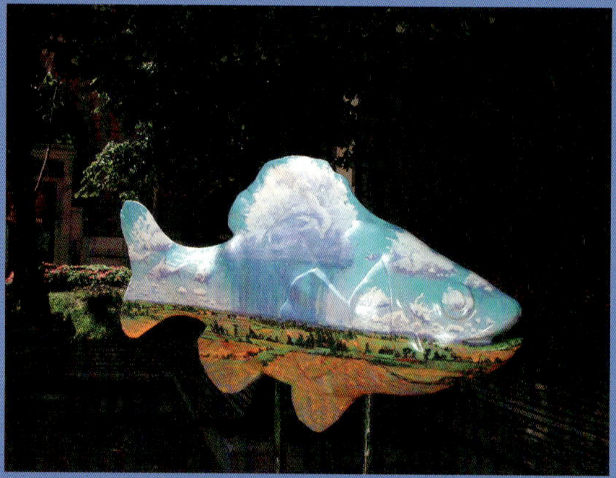

MISTER FISH
Mary Beth Akre
Ballard Spahr Andrews & Ingersoll, LLP

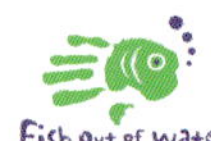

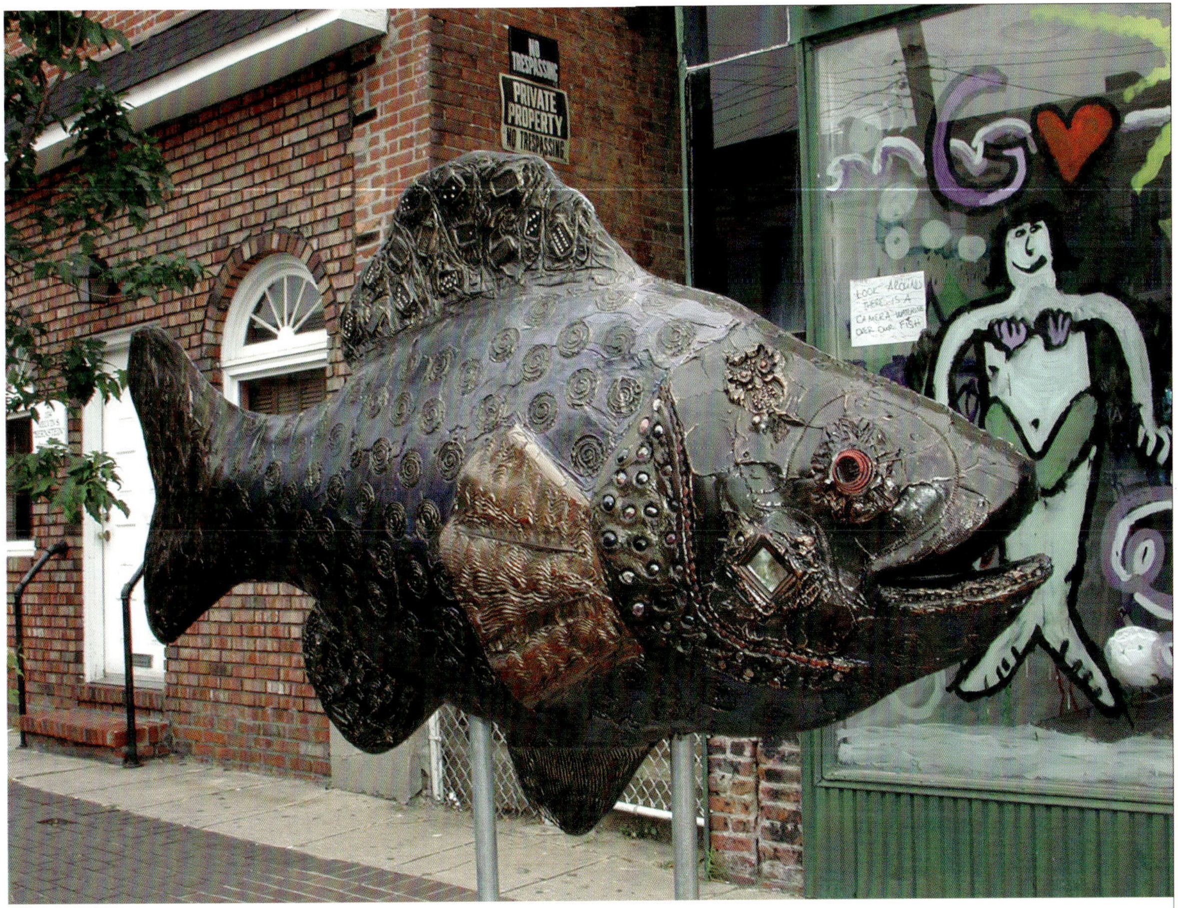

FISH OF DREAMS
Jacquie Shane
Hampden Family Center

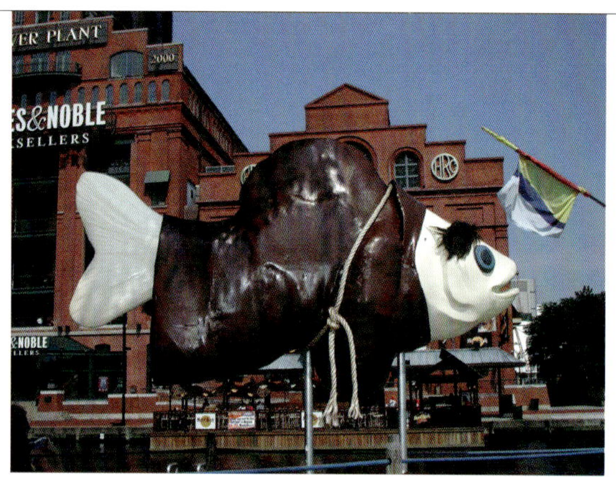

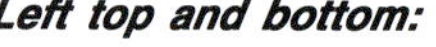

Left top and bottom:

MONK FISH

Courtney Blake Sinn

National Aquarium in Baltimore

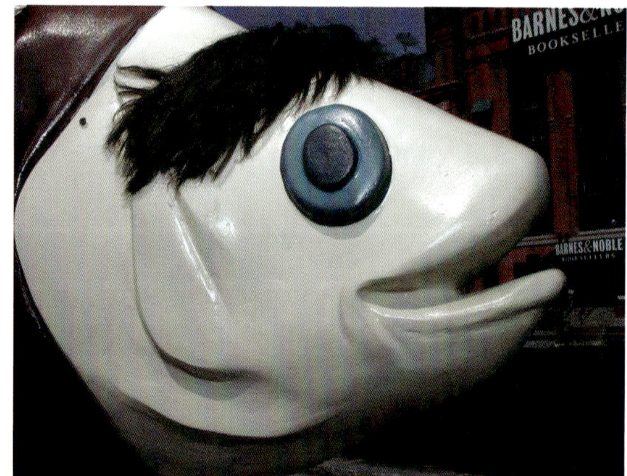

Right:

LOOKS LIKE RAIN

Sharon Roslund

WJZ-TV

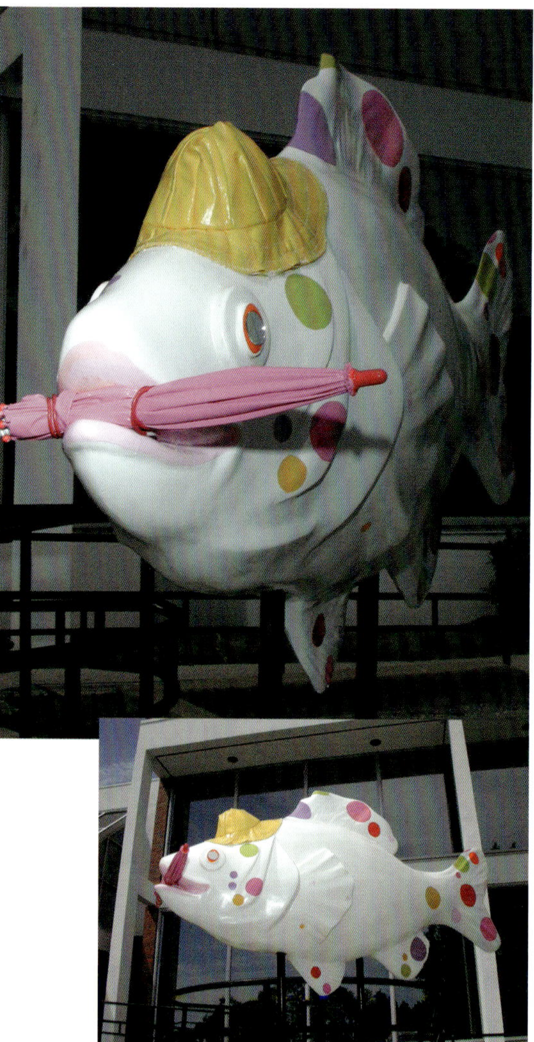

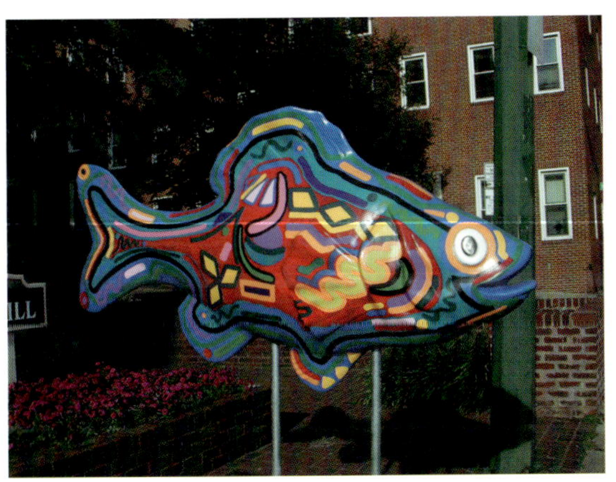

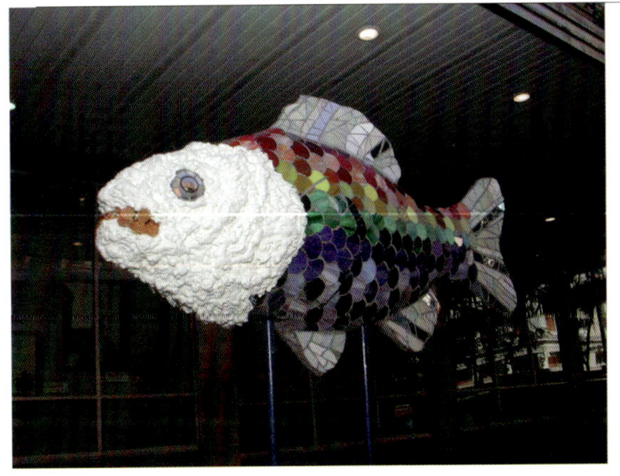

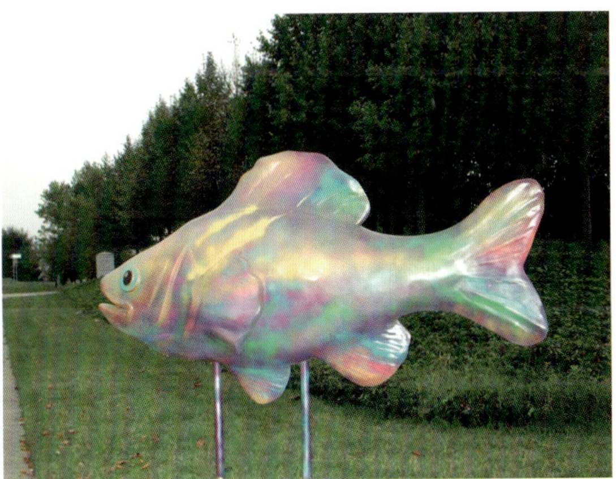

Clockwise, from top left:

WISH FISH
Loren Newmark
The Annie E. Casey Foundation for the children and families of East Baltimore

RAINBOW TROUT
Louisa Rettew and Mary Lyons
Southern Management Corporation

RAINBOW CONNECTION
Carolyn Hartman
Katiah Development, Inc. & Ashley Custom Homes

FISH ON THEIR WAY DOWN

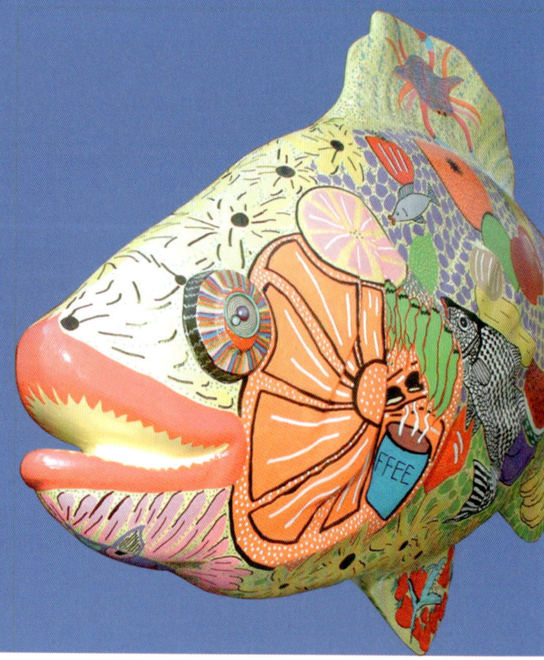

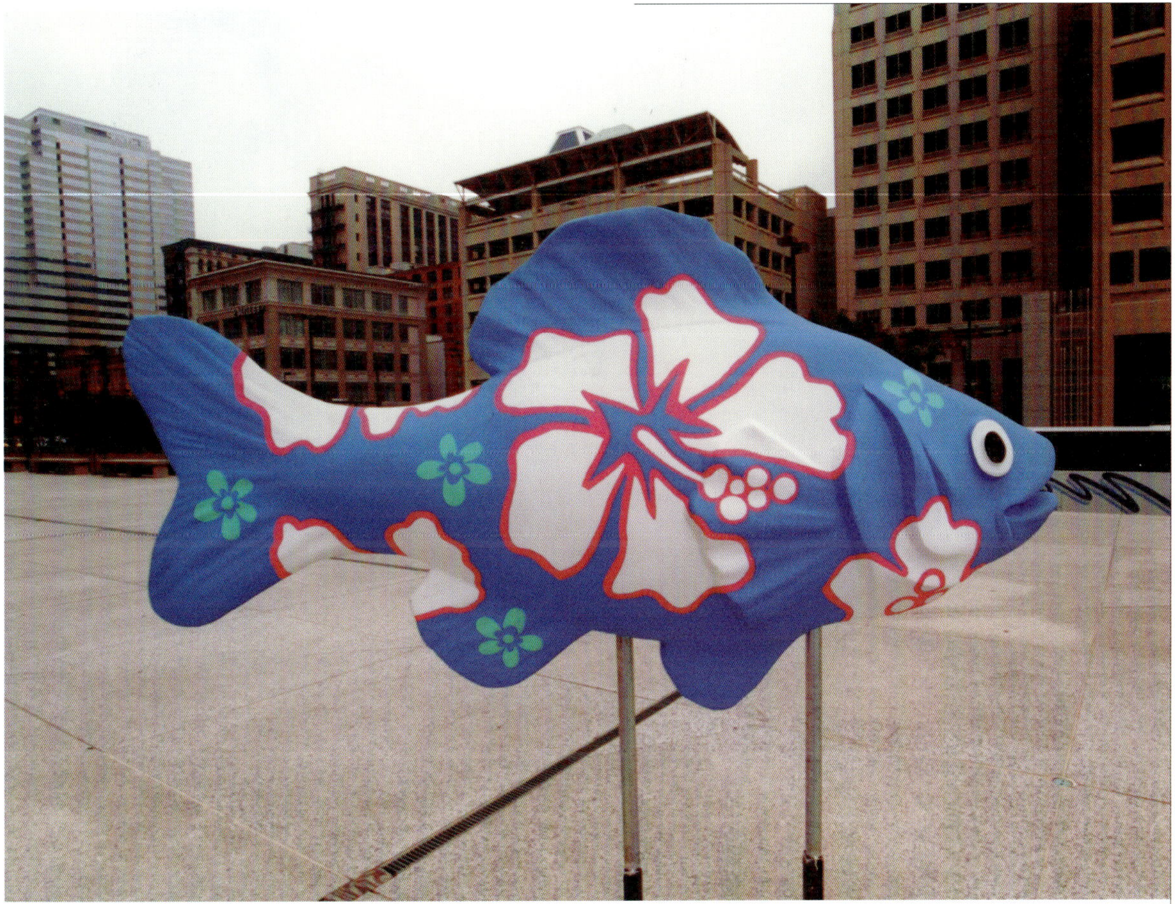

ALOHA MAHI MAHI

Lisa Hutton

Legg Mason Inc.

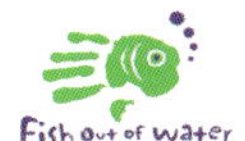

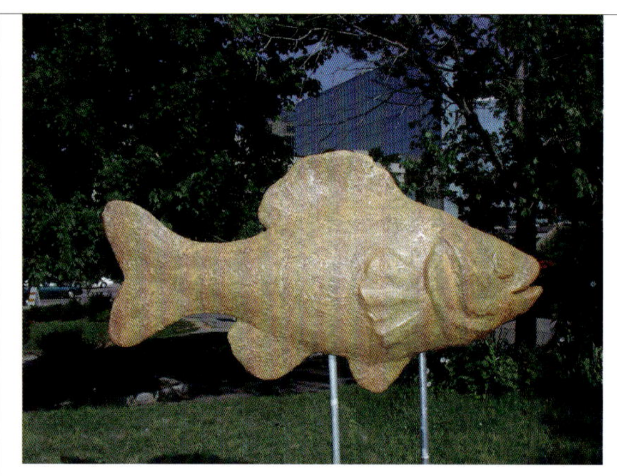

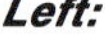

Left:

FISH FRY
Anthony Cervino
McCormick & Co. Inc. / Old Bay

Right:

TUNA ROLL WITH ROE
Mike W. Anthony &
Sarah Barnes
Struever Bros. Eccles &
Rouse, Inc.

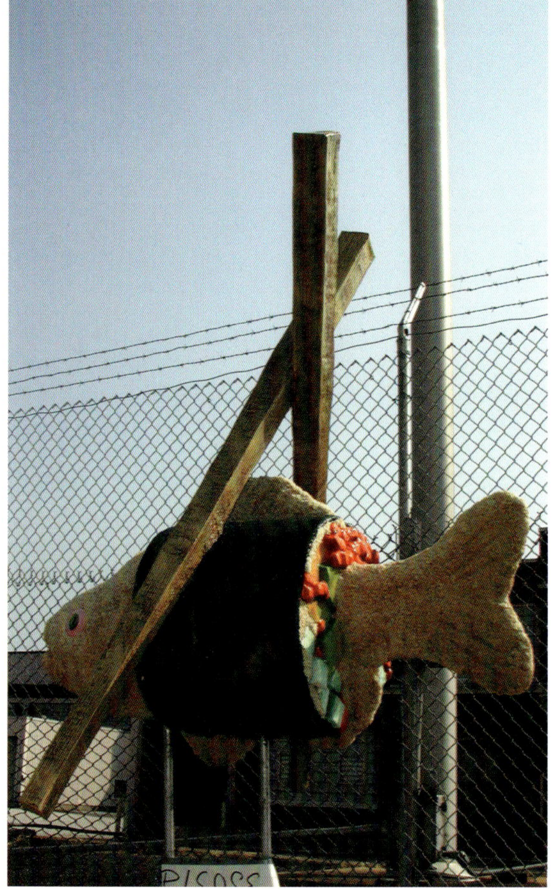

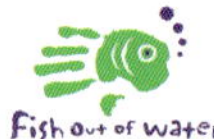

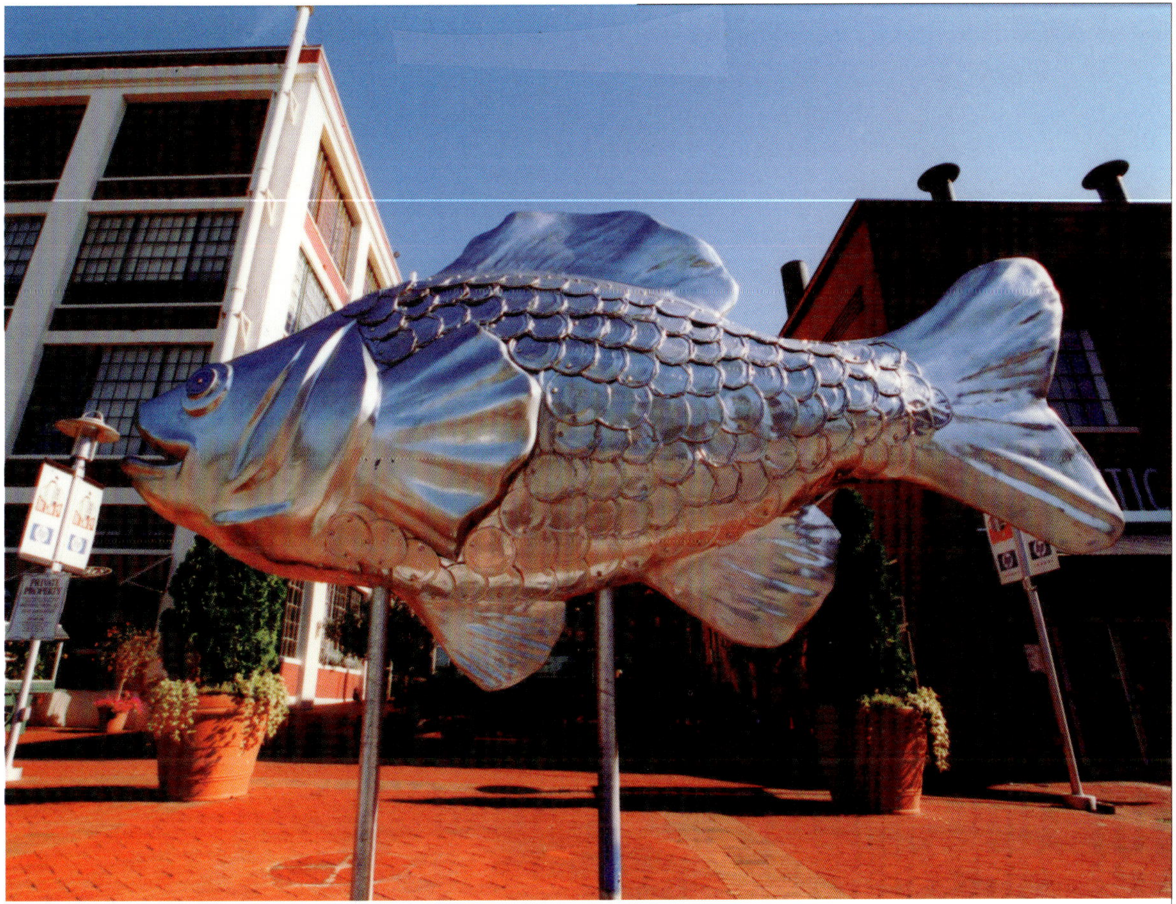

TIN CANNED TUNA

Bobby Hansson

Struever Bros. Eccles & Rouse, Inc.

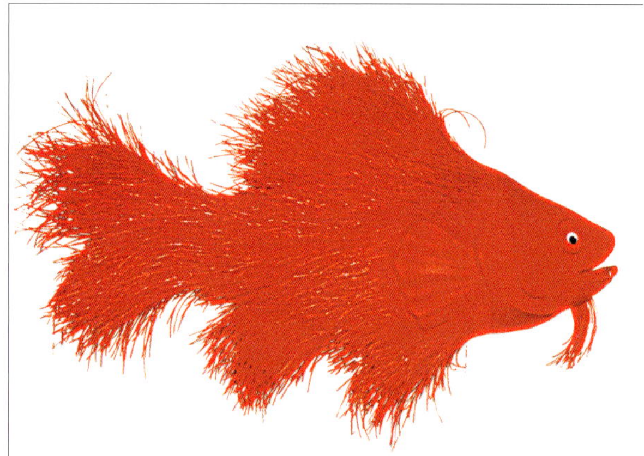

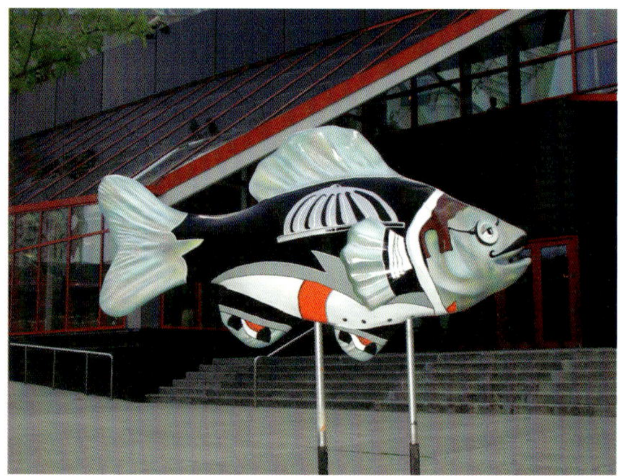

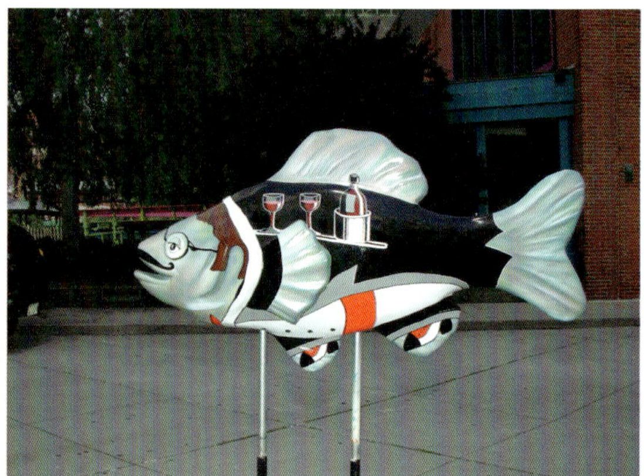

Left:

ORANGE RUFFIAN
Steve Ziger & Hollis McCracken
Darielle Lineham

Right top and bottom:

AT YOUR SERFISH
Gail Holliday
The Classic Catering People

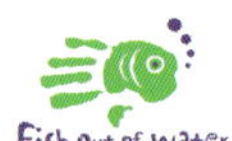

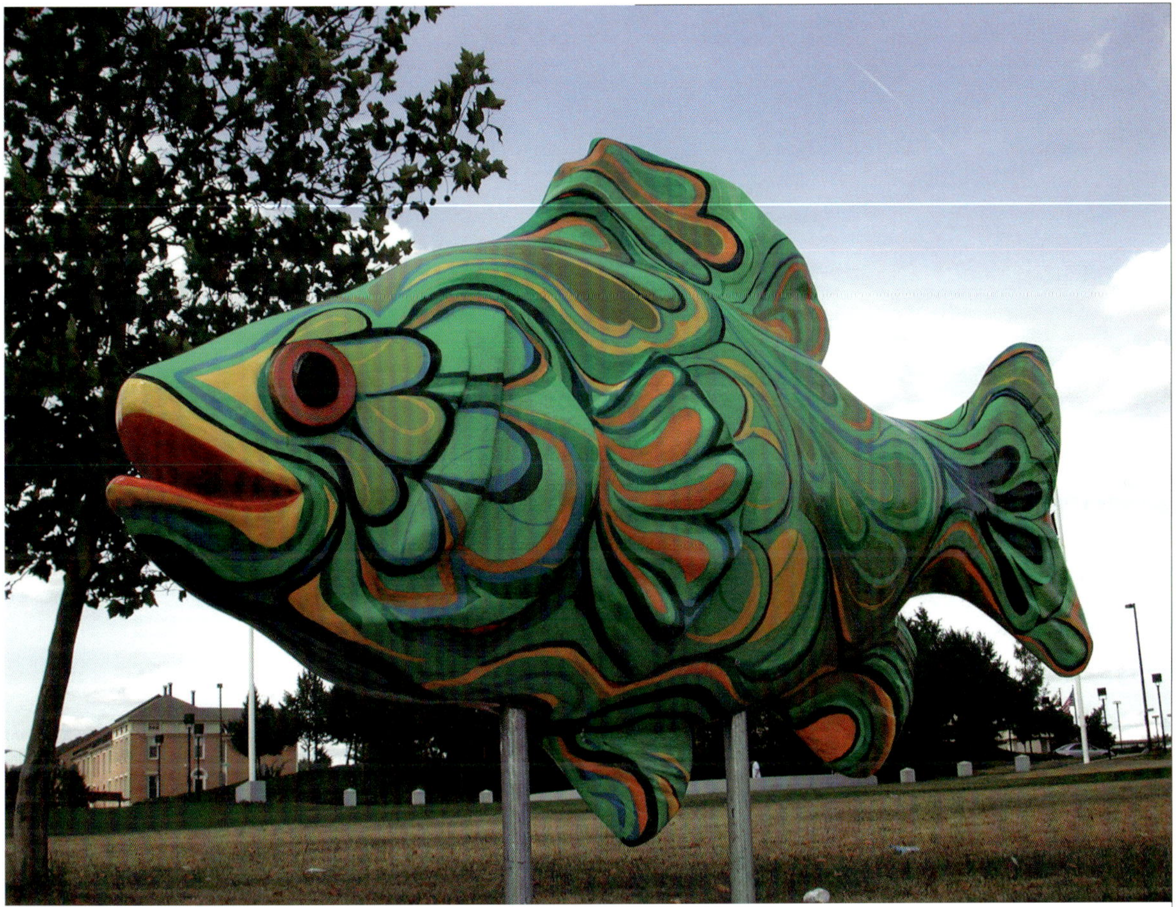

FLORENTINA
Dorothy Fix
Fish Out of Water

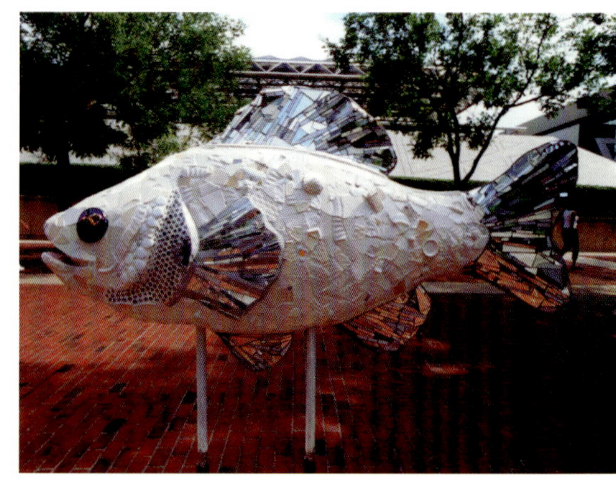

Clockwise, from top right:

WHITEFISH AND LOX
Leslie F. Miller
Harry and Jeanette
Weinberg Foundation

YOU ARE WHAT YOU EAT (SEAFOOD DIET)
Jonathan West
France-Merrick Foundation

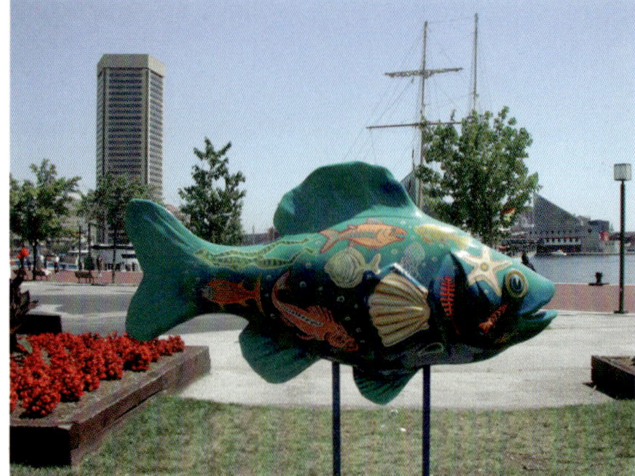

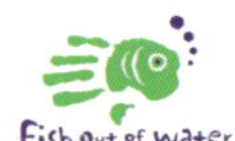

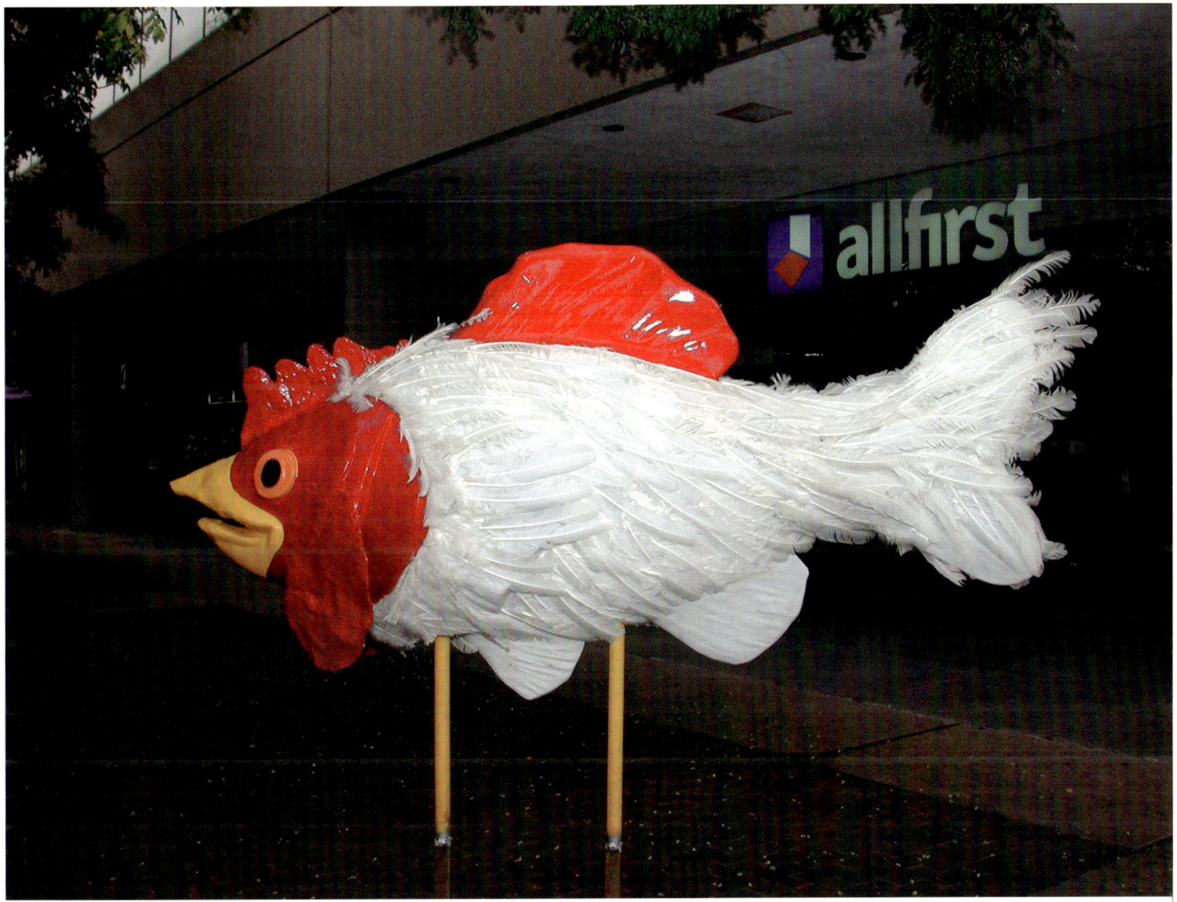

CHICKEN OF THE SEA
Nina Rutledge
93.1 WPOC/Clear Channel Worldwide

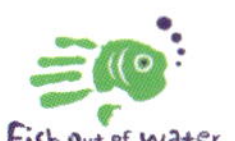

GREAT AMERICAN SEAFOOD CHALLENGE

Barbara Cox

Pepsi-Cola

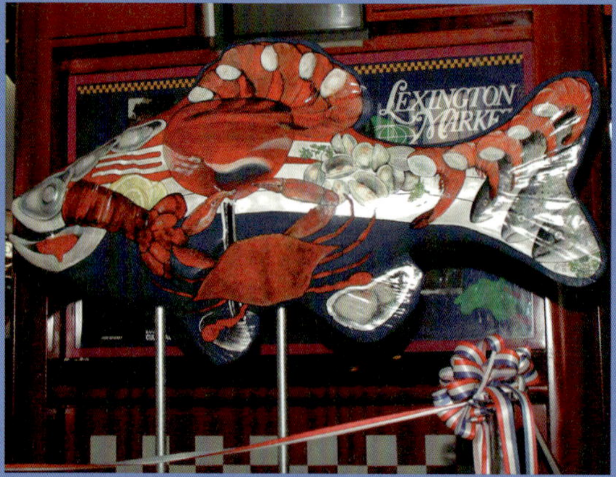

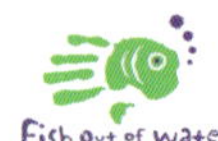

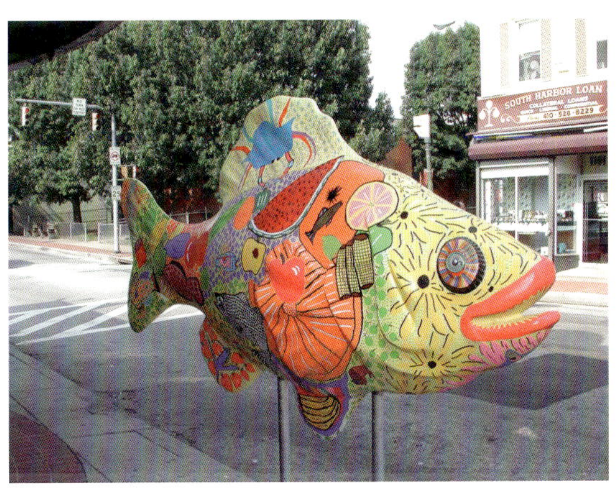

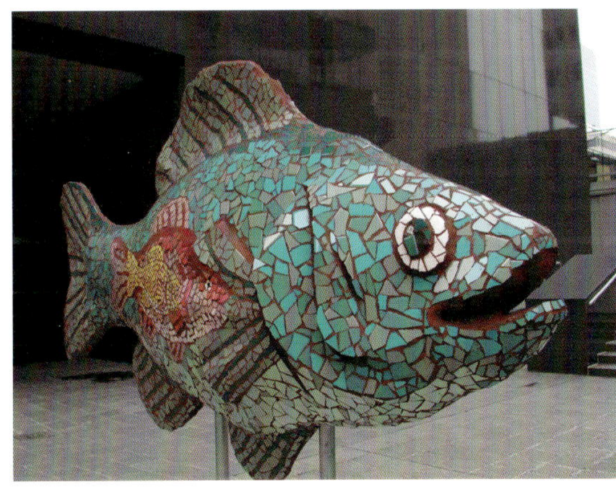

Left:

FISH MARKET
Susan Fernandez-Janczak
Historic Federal Hill Main Street and Cross Street Market Merchants' Assc.

Right:

FOOD FISH
Mae Lucier
Shapiro, Sher & Guinot

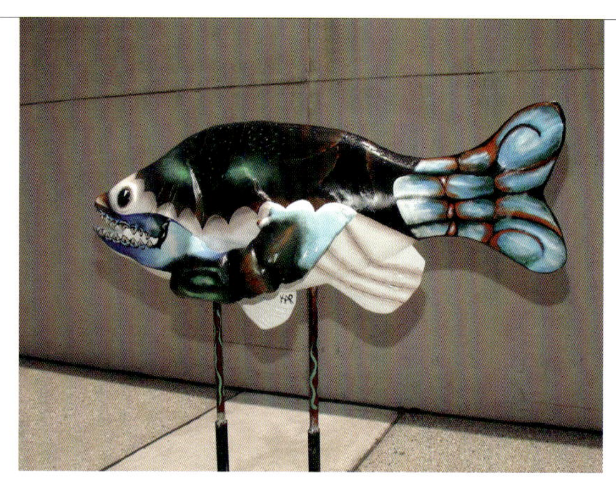

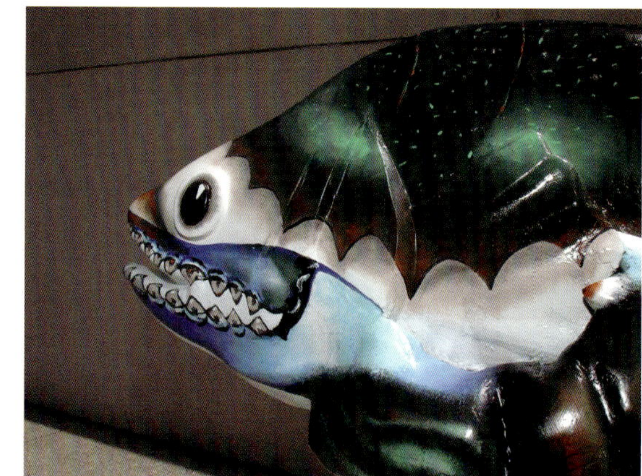

Top left and right:

CRABISH
Kevin Richardson
ARAMARK Sports
& Entertainment

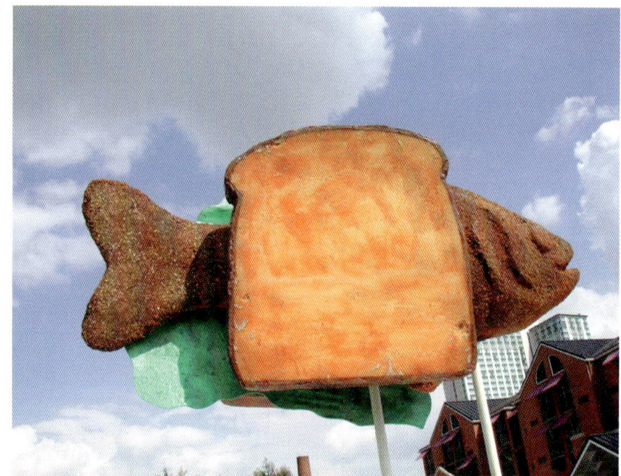

Bottom:

FISH SANDWICH
Jennifer Stuart Watson
Fish Out of Water

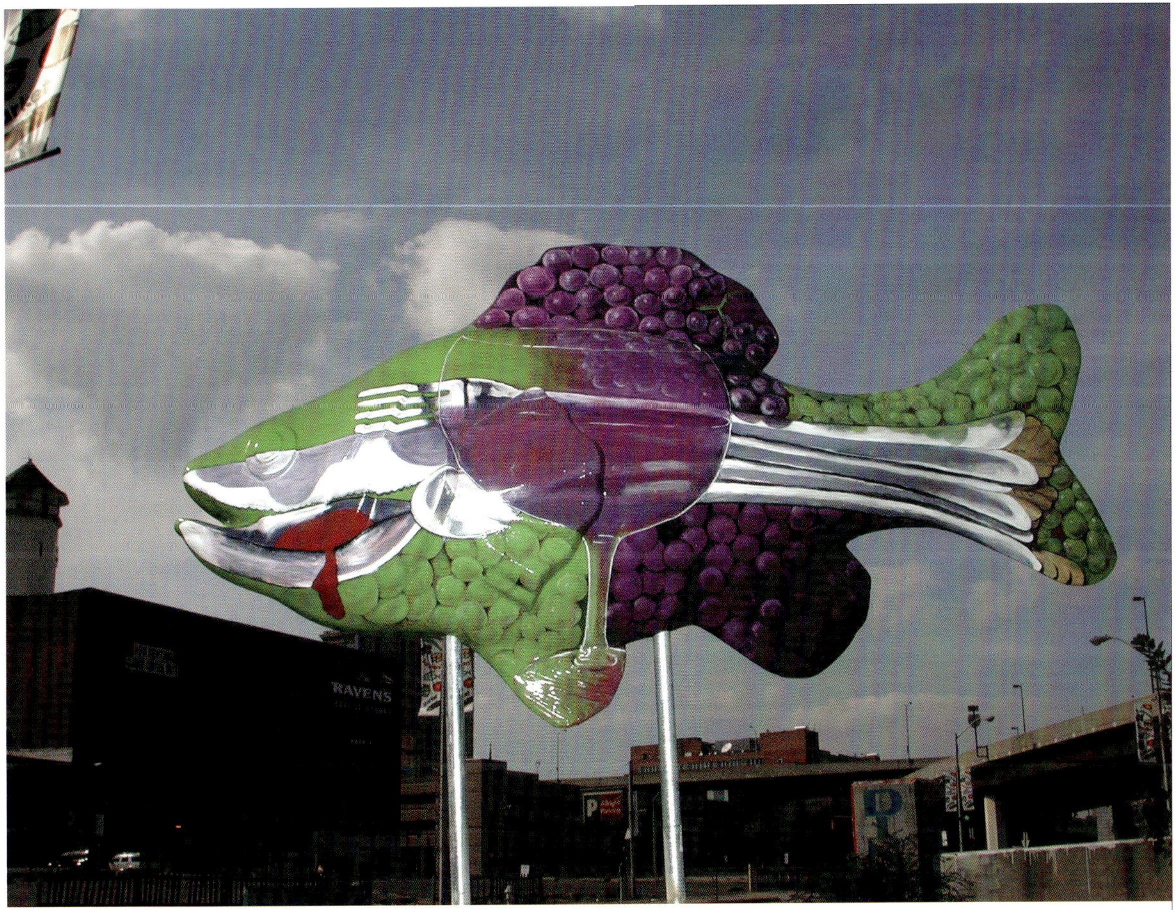

BOUILLABASS

Barbara Cox

Esther S. Pearlstone Foundation/
Restaurant Association of Maryland (RAM)

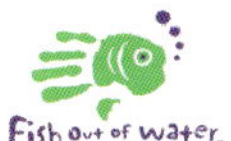

FISH AROUND TOWN

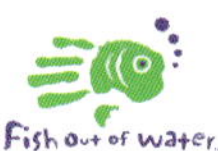

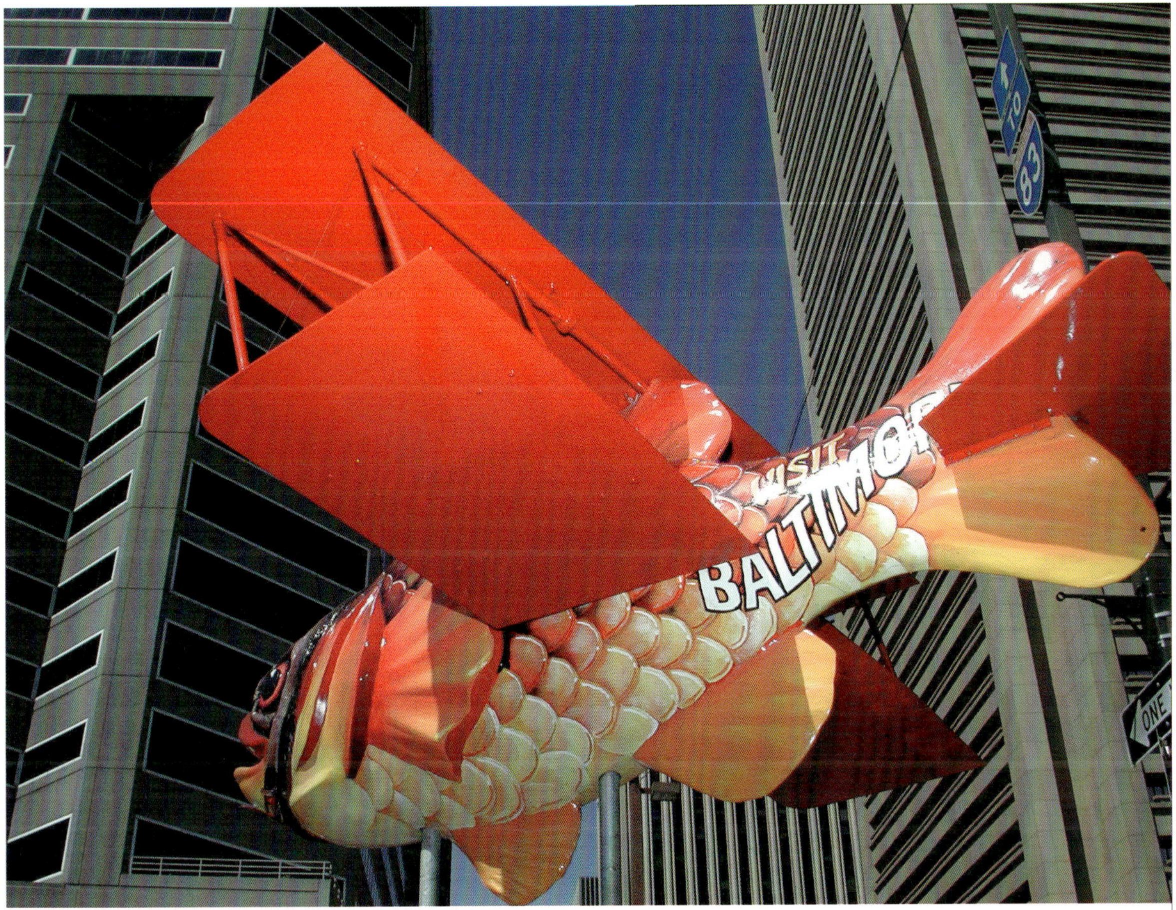

ICHTHYOLOGICAL BALTIMORE AERIALIST

Jerry R. Arnold, Sharon Blackburn, Mitch Heinz, Elizabeth Slaterbeck, Jim Durham

Baltimore Area Convention and Visitors Association

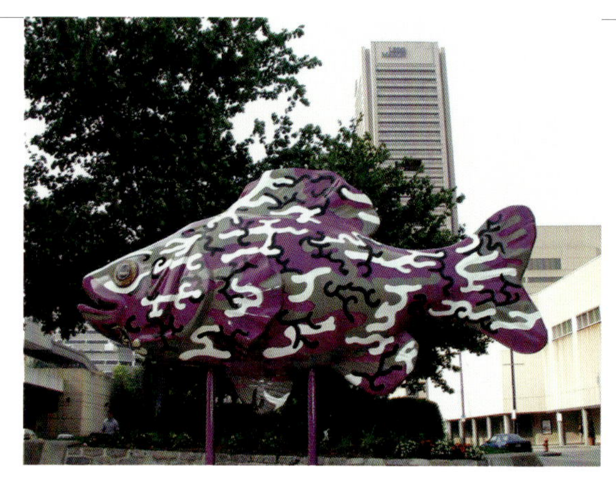

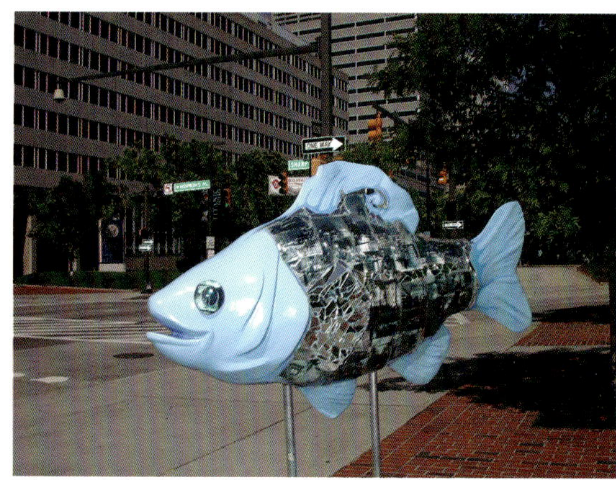

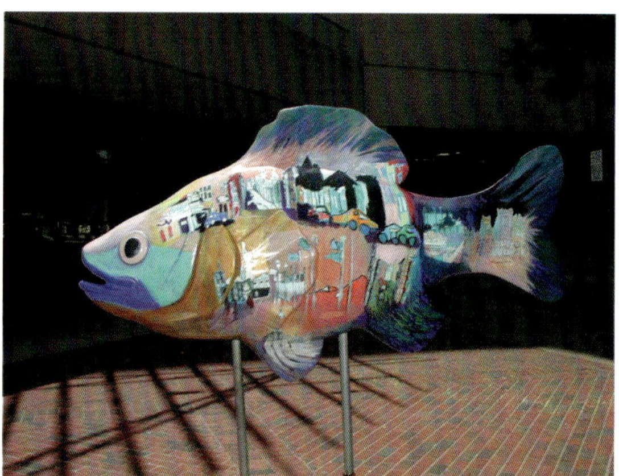

Clockwise, from top left:

RAVENOUS CAMOFISH
Jonathan West
Zurich Small Business

3AM FISH
Marc Elzey
Comfort Link

FISHING FOR COMPLIMENTS
Cooper Hanson
Verizon

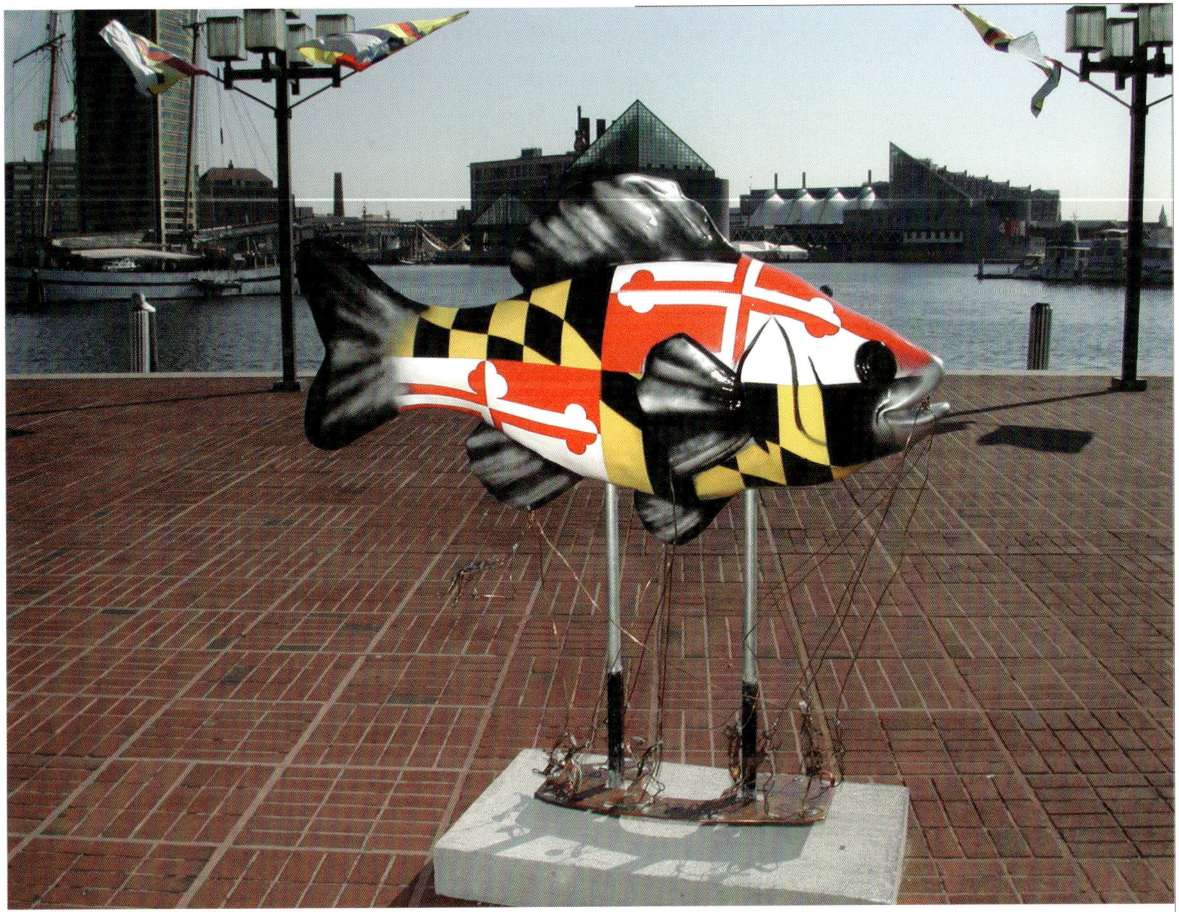

MARYLAND DAY PARADE
George Lucas
SunTrust Bank

Clockwise, from top left:

THE ALLURE OF BALTIMORE
Mike W. Anthony & Sarah Barnes
The Rouse Company

SUSQUEHANNA DAM JUMPER
Brent Crothers
The Cordish Company

FISH ROW
Kylis P. Winborne
American Skyline Insurance Company

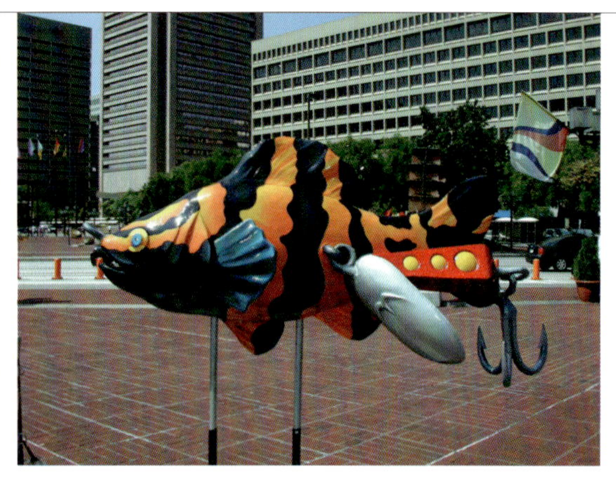

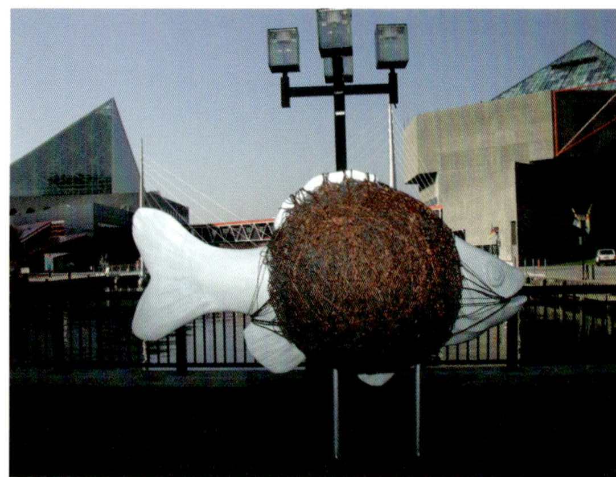

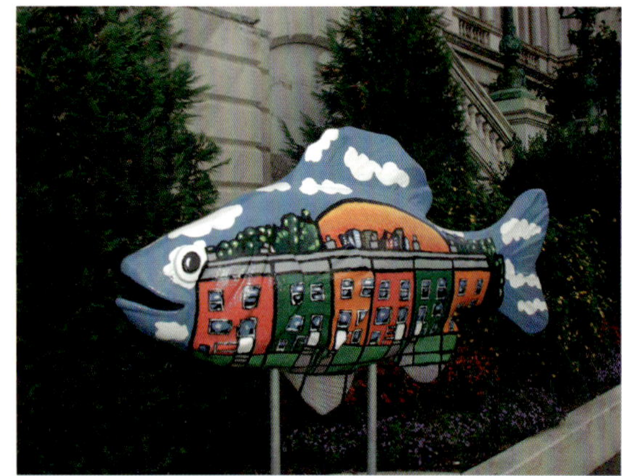

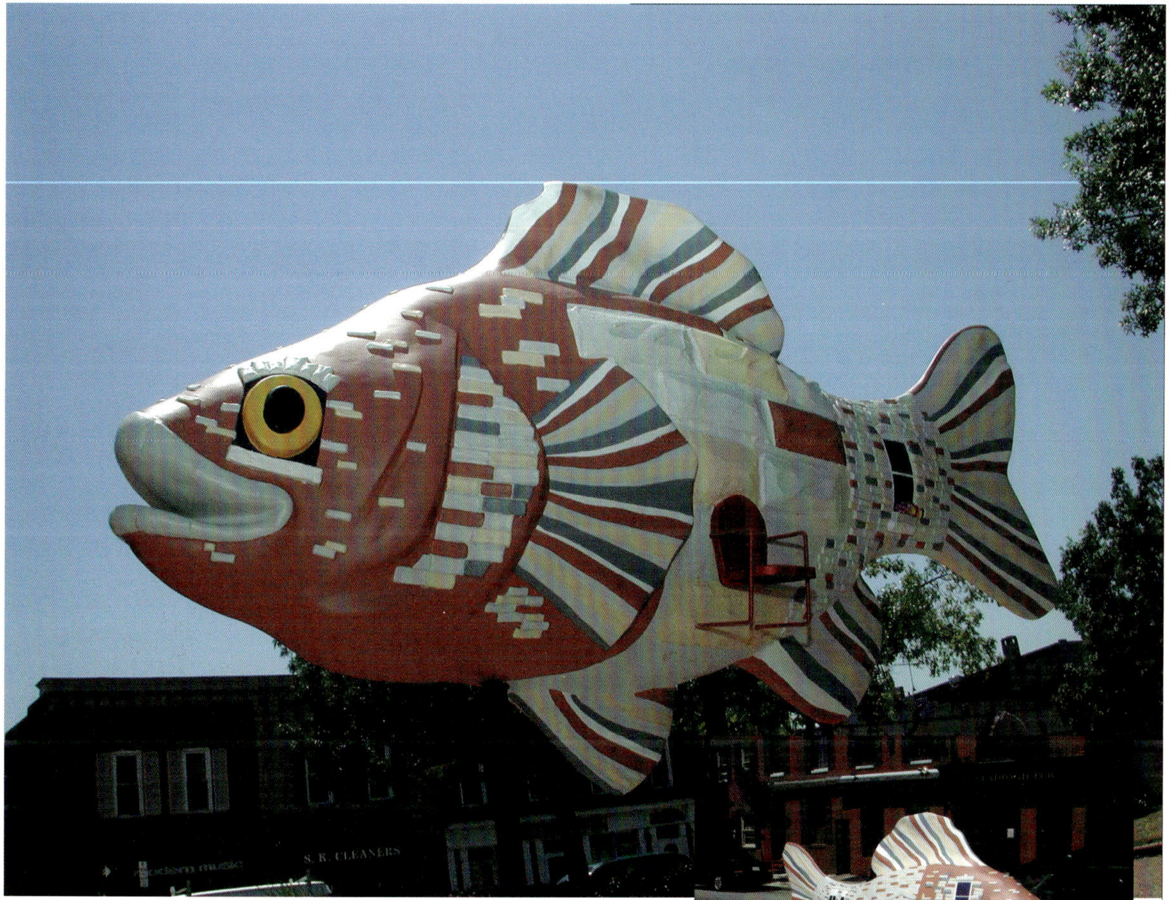

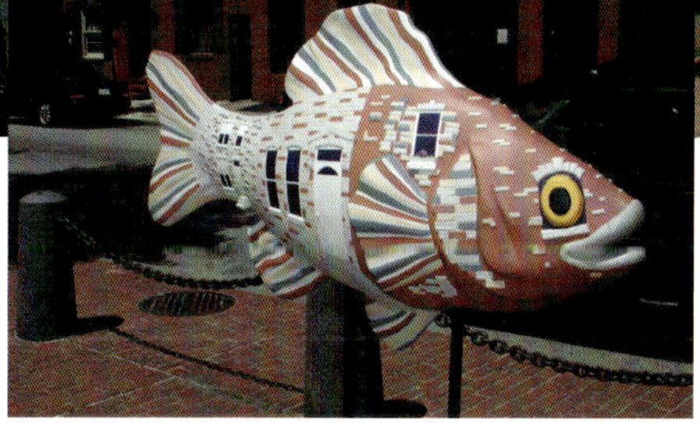

FORMSTONE ROEHOUSE FISH

Kristine Yuki Aono

France-Merrick Foundation

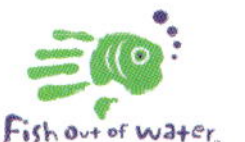

Clockwise, from top left:

ROCKIN LADY BALTIMORE
Joann Larrimore
Lord Baltimore Capital Corporation

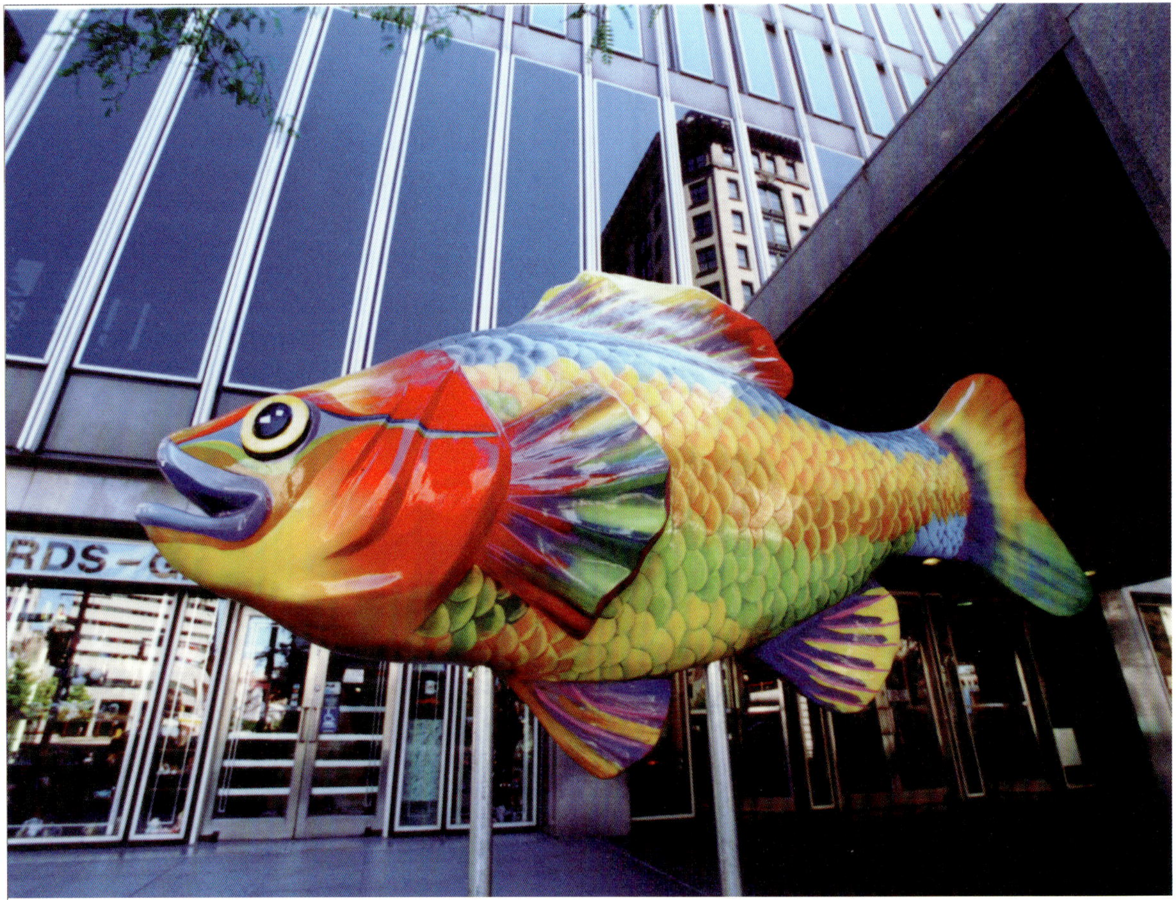

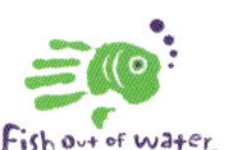

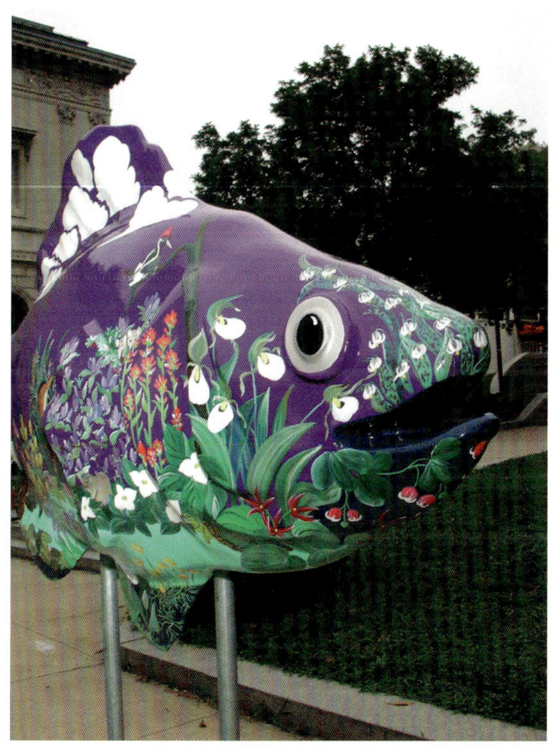

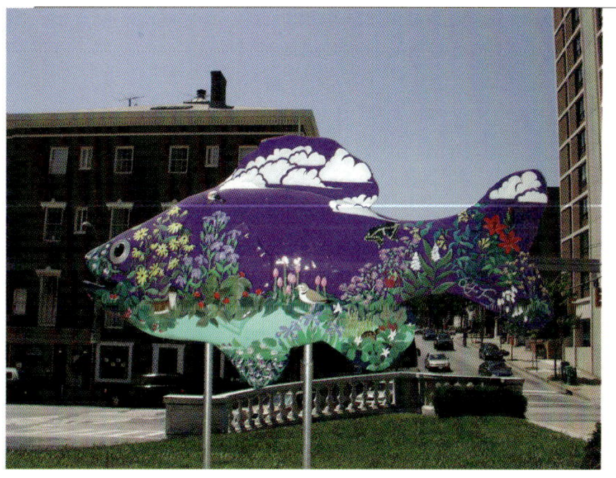

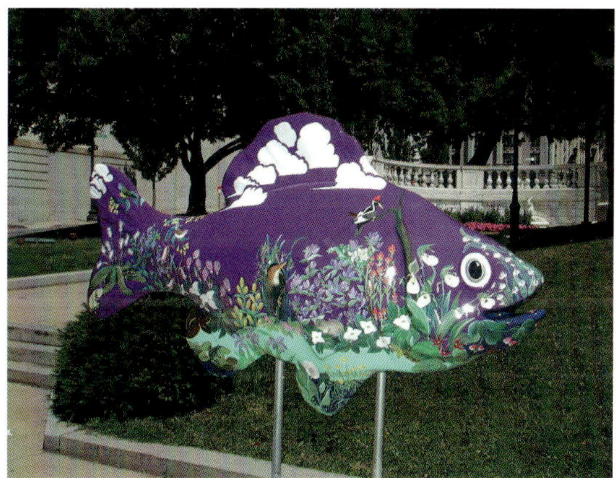

THE ROCK GARDEN: MARYLAND'S ENDANGERED FLORA & FAUNA

Rufus Toomey

The Whiting-Turner Contracting Company

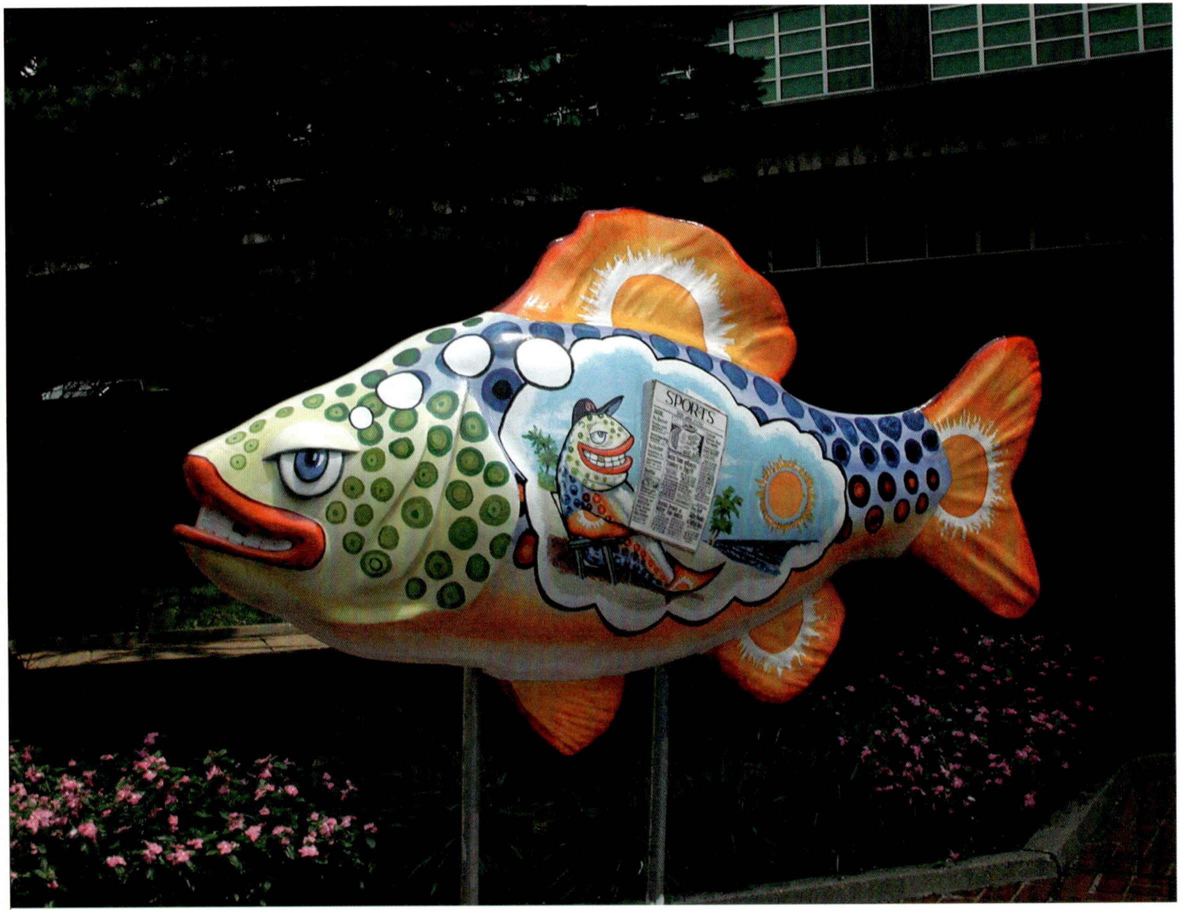

THE SUNFISH
Kevin Kal Kallaugher
The Baltimore Sun

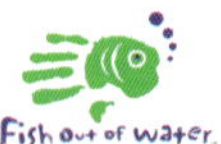

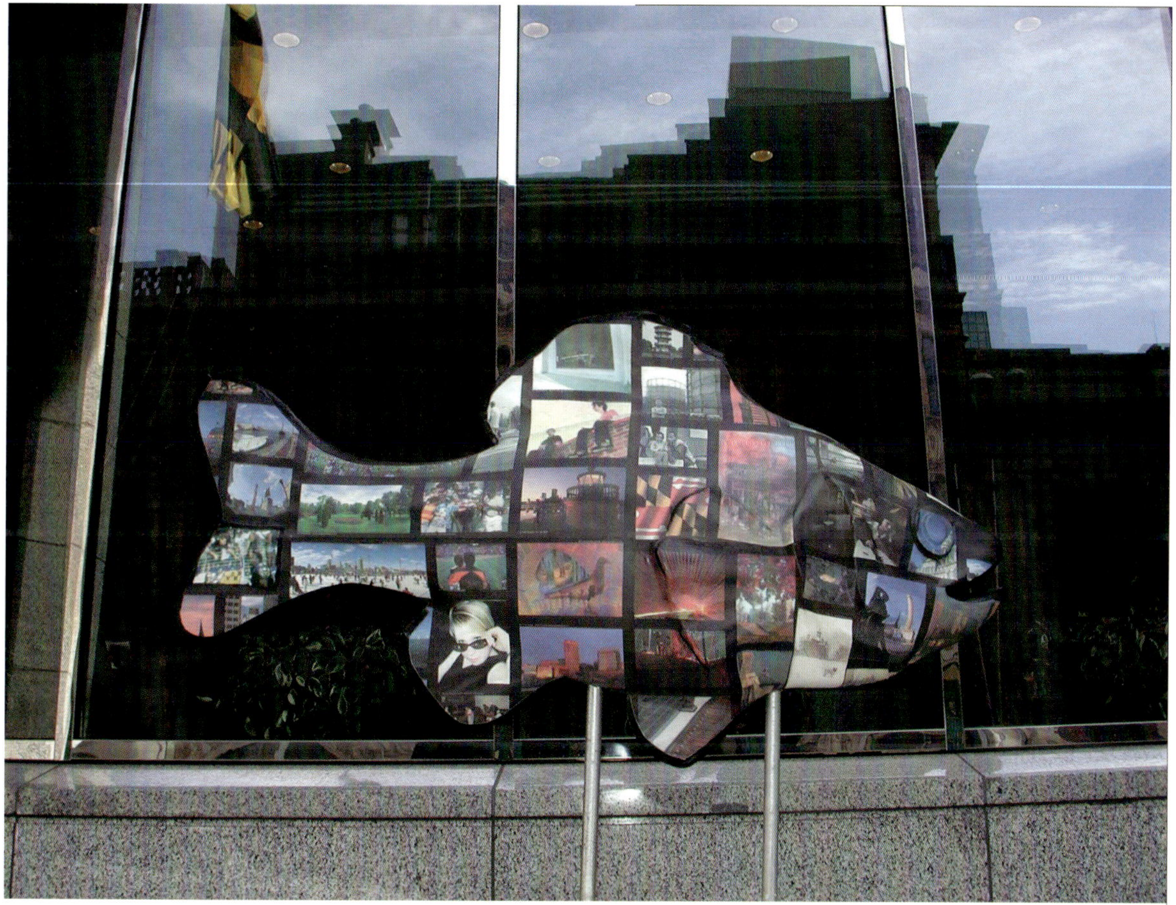

FISH EYE
American Society of Media Photographers
Downtown Partnership of Baltimore

ROCK FISH
Ron Good
Greater Baltimore
Medical Center

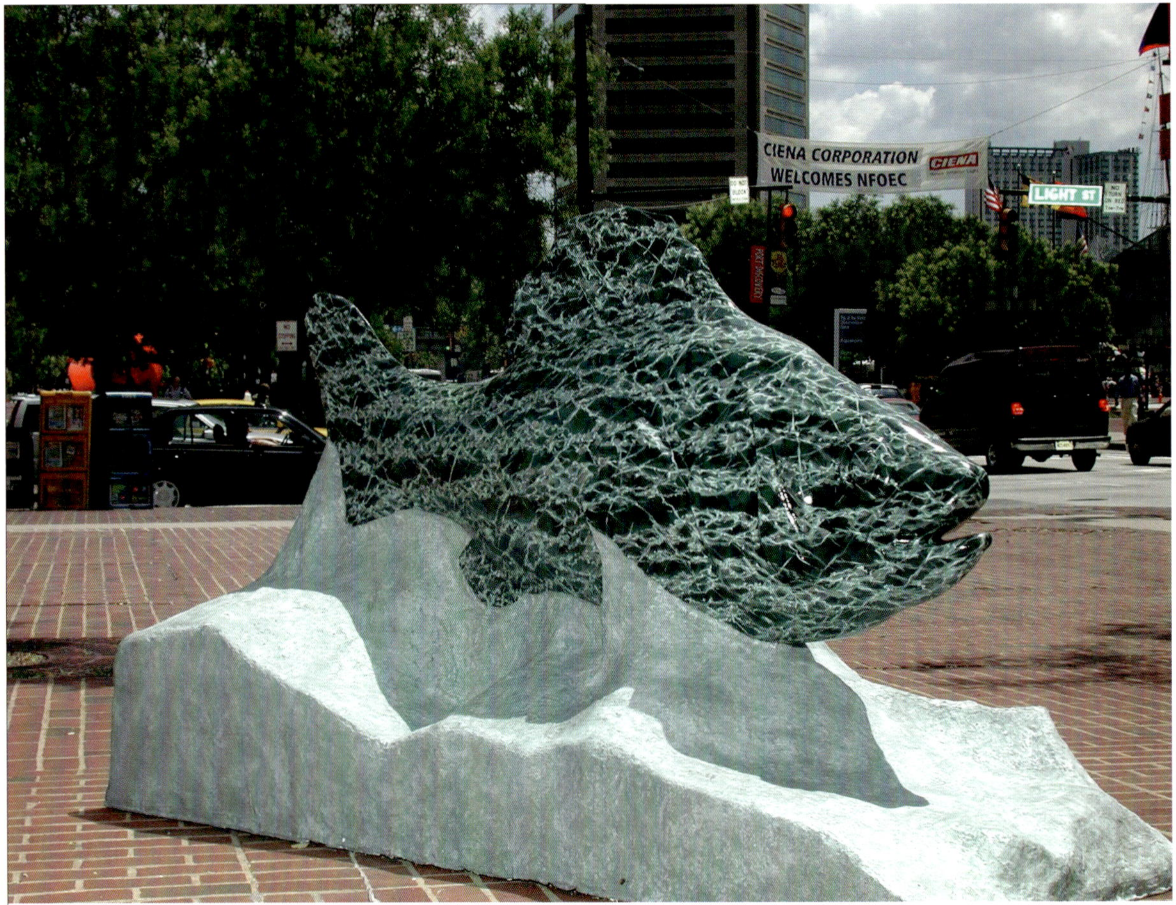

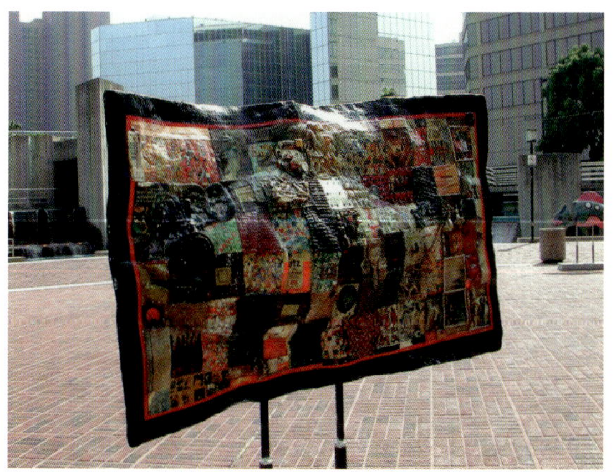

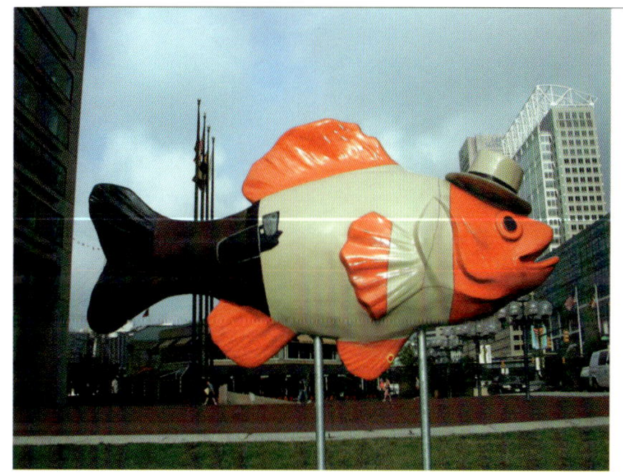

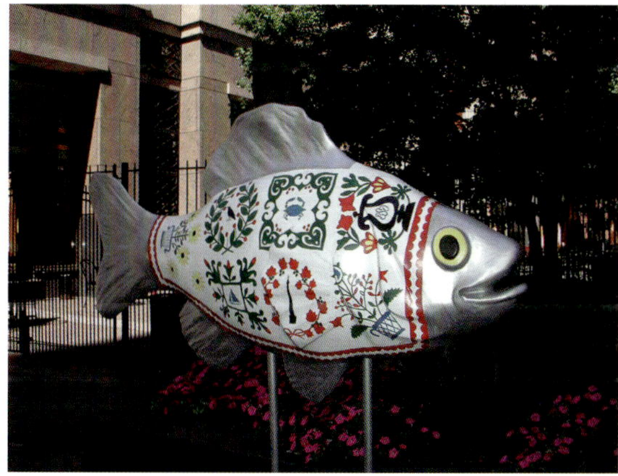

Clockwise, from top left:

BALTIMORE QUILT FISH
David Bacharach
Comcast Cable

STATE GROUPER
Jerry Edwards, Jr.
Harry and Jeanette Weinberg Foundation

BALTIMORE ALBUM QUILT
James Drake Iams
Deutsche Banc Alex. Brown

Clockwise, from top left:

POE FISH / FISH OUT OF JOHN WATERS
Spoon Popkin
Tremont Suite Hotels

FISH-TOGRAPH
Joel L. Meneses
Carter & Burgess Consultants, Inc. and Family and Friends

WHERE WE CAME FROM
Espi Frazier
NAACP National Headquarters

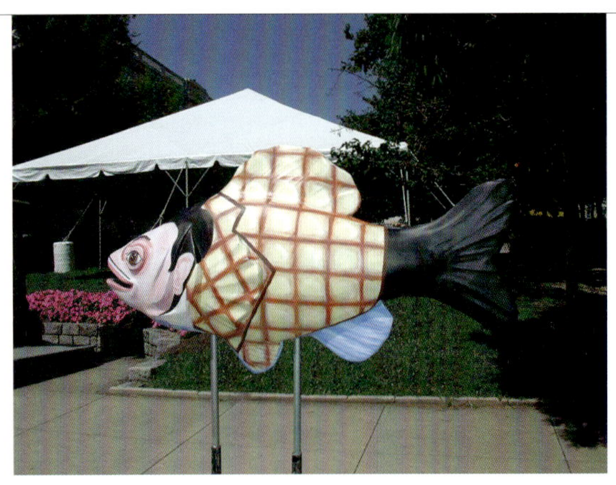

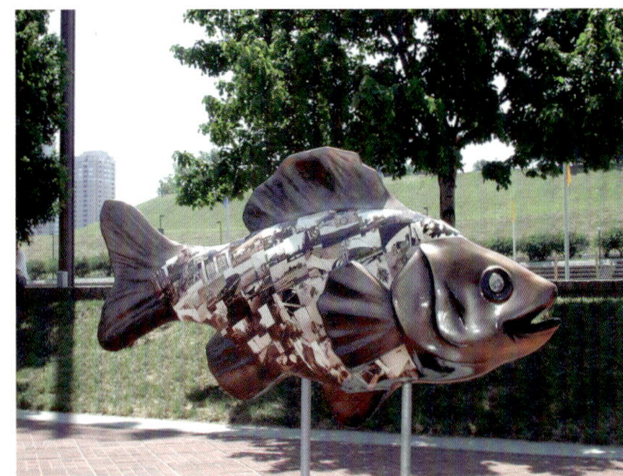

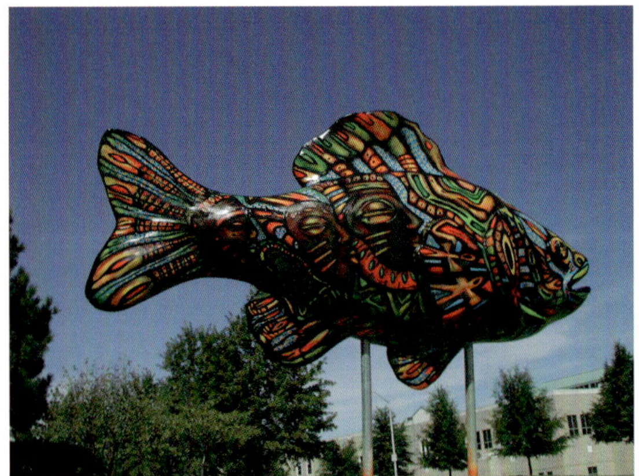

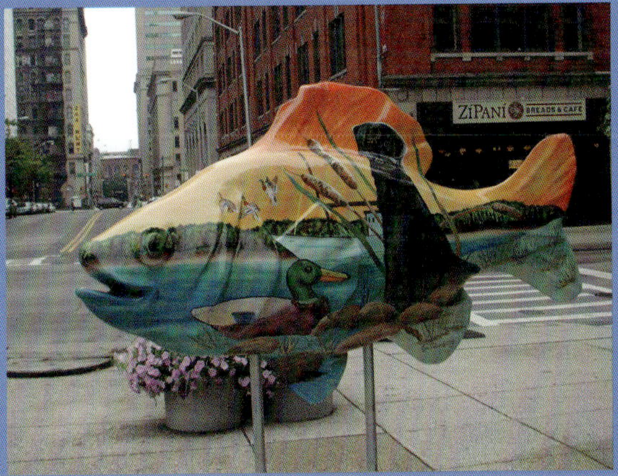

RETRIEVE THE BAY

Mark W. Anthony

Fish Out of Water

FISH WITH RHYTHM

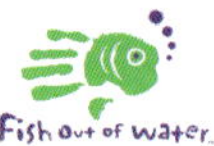

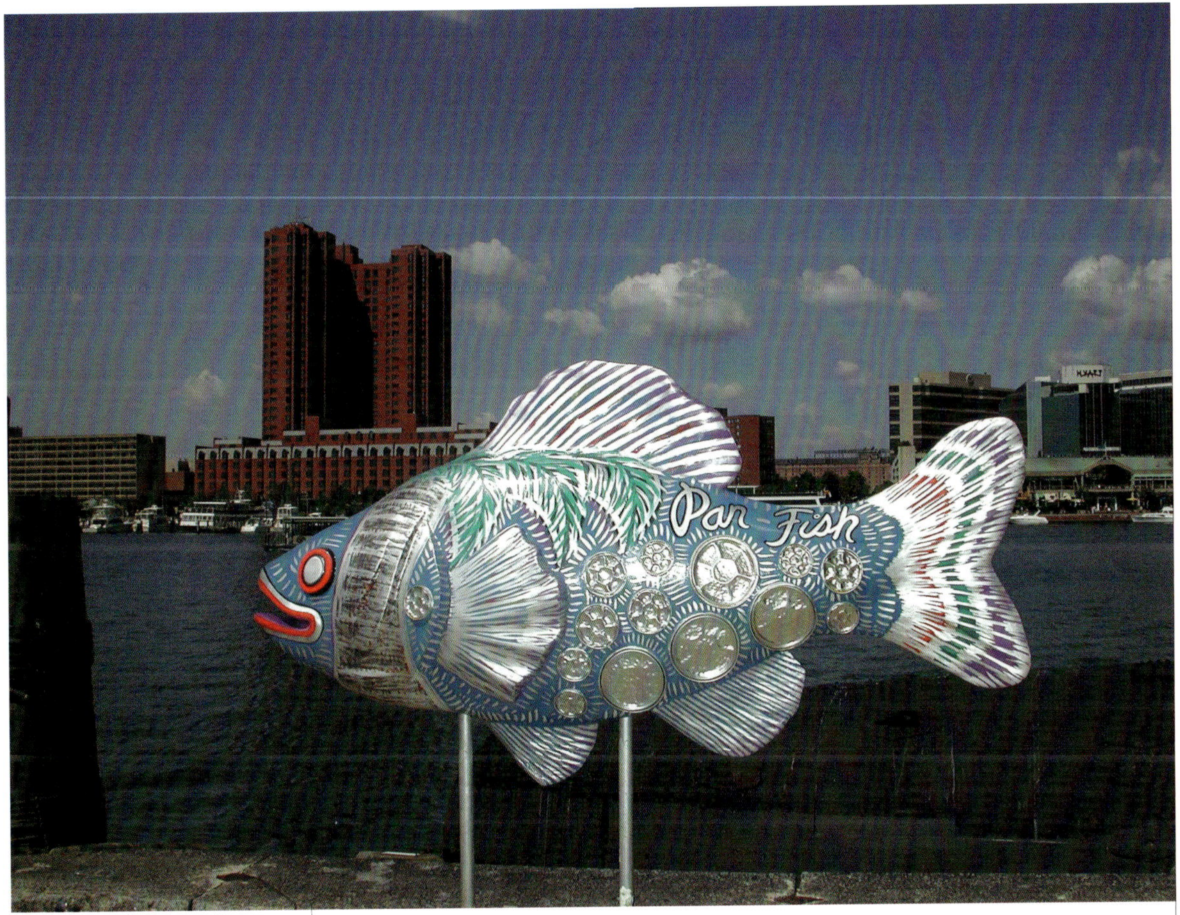

PAN FISH
Anne Brant Stack
US Filter

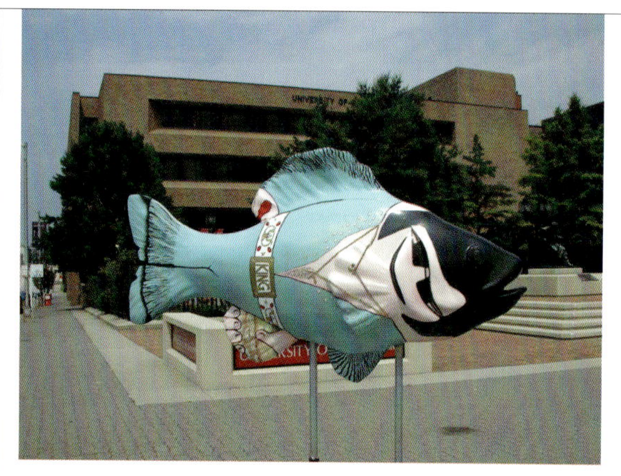

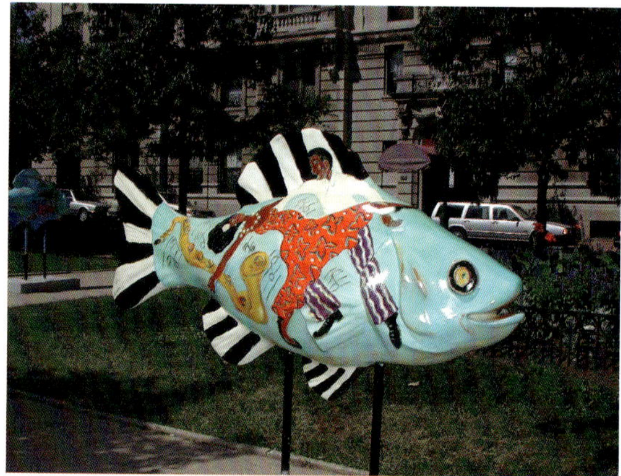

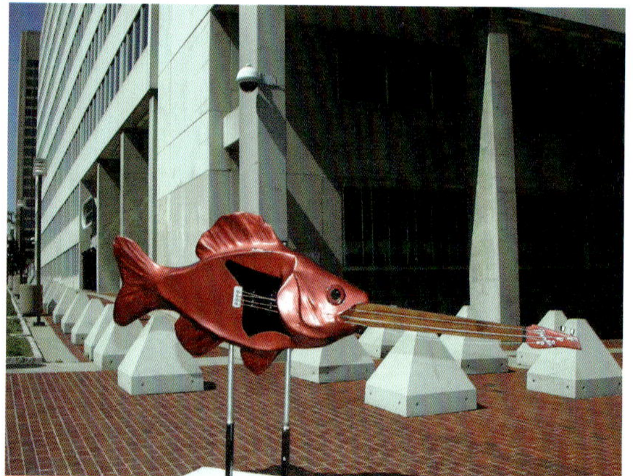

Clockwise, from top left:

ELFISH—THE KING
Barbara Cox
Kaplan & Kaplan, P.A.

TUNE A FISH
Mark Barry
France-Merrick Foundation

TUNA GUITAR
Steven Weitzman
Kramon & Graham, P.A.

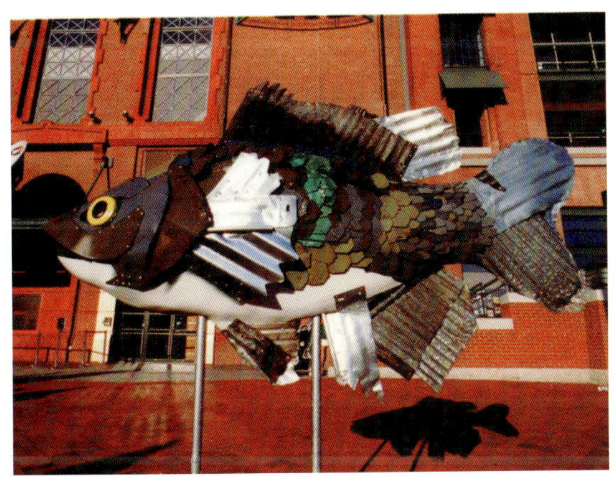

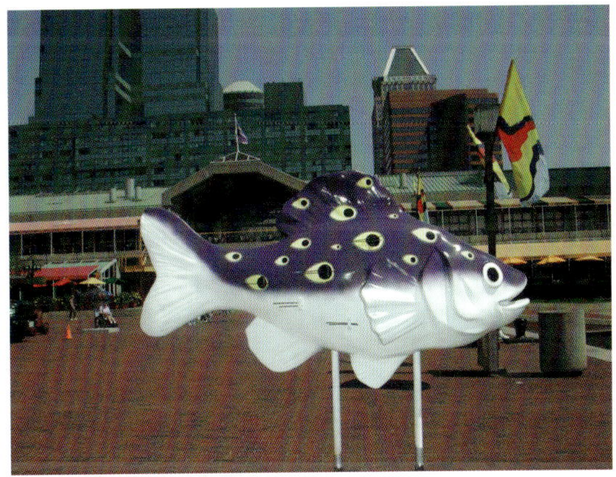

Clockwise, from top left:

STEEL DRUM (CRAPPIE METAL)
Adam Bradley
Design Collective, Inc.

PLAYING FISH SCALE
Denham Ikemefuna Fassett
Manekin, LLC

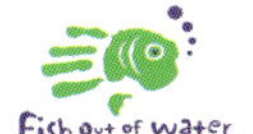

(THAT'S WHY THEY CALL IT THE) BLUESFISH

Gary Jameson

Heery International, Inc.

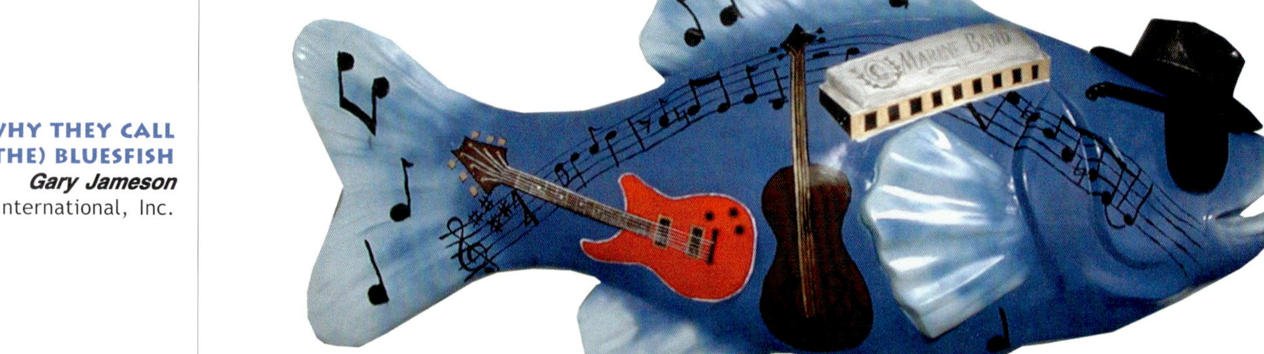

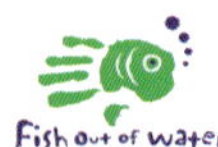

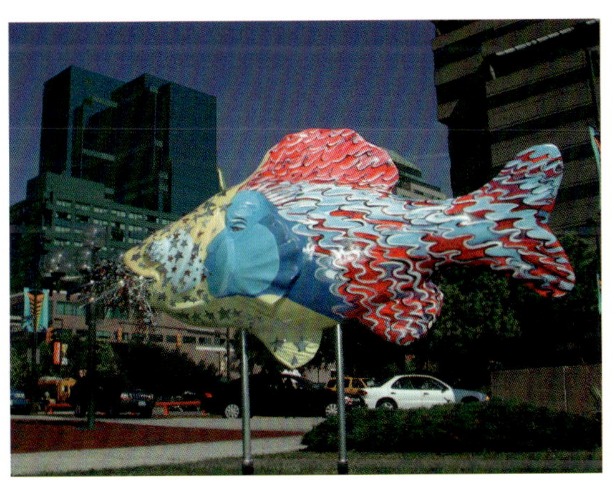

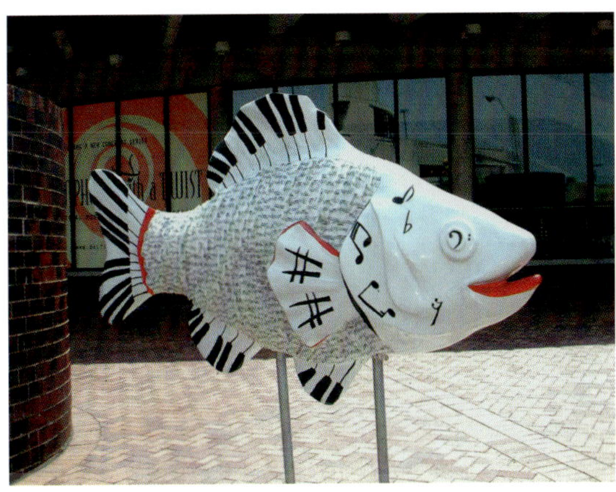

Left:

ZEPHYR
Paula Phillips
Besche Oil Co.

Right:

JOHANN SEA-BASS-TIAN BACH
Sandra Zylberman
SunTrust Bank

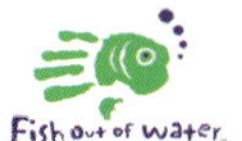

FISH AT WORK

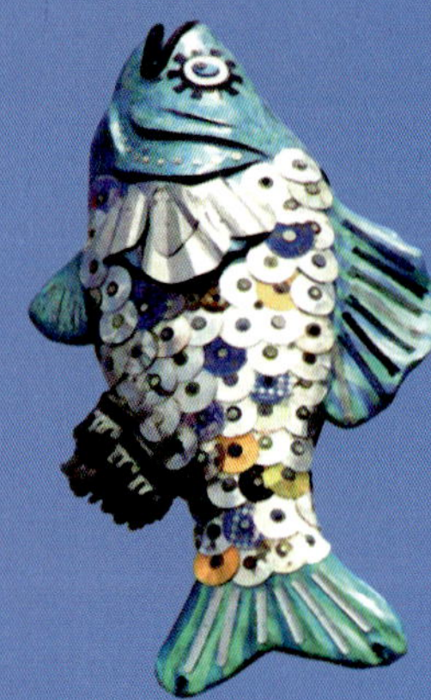

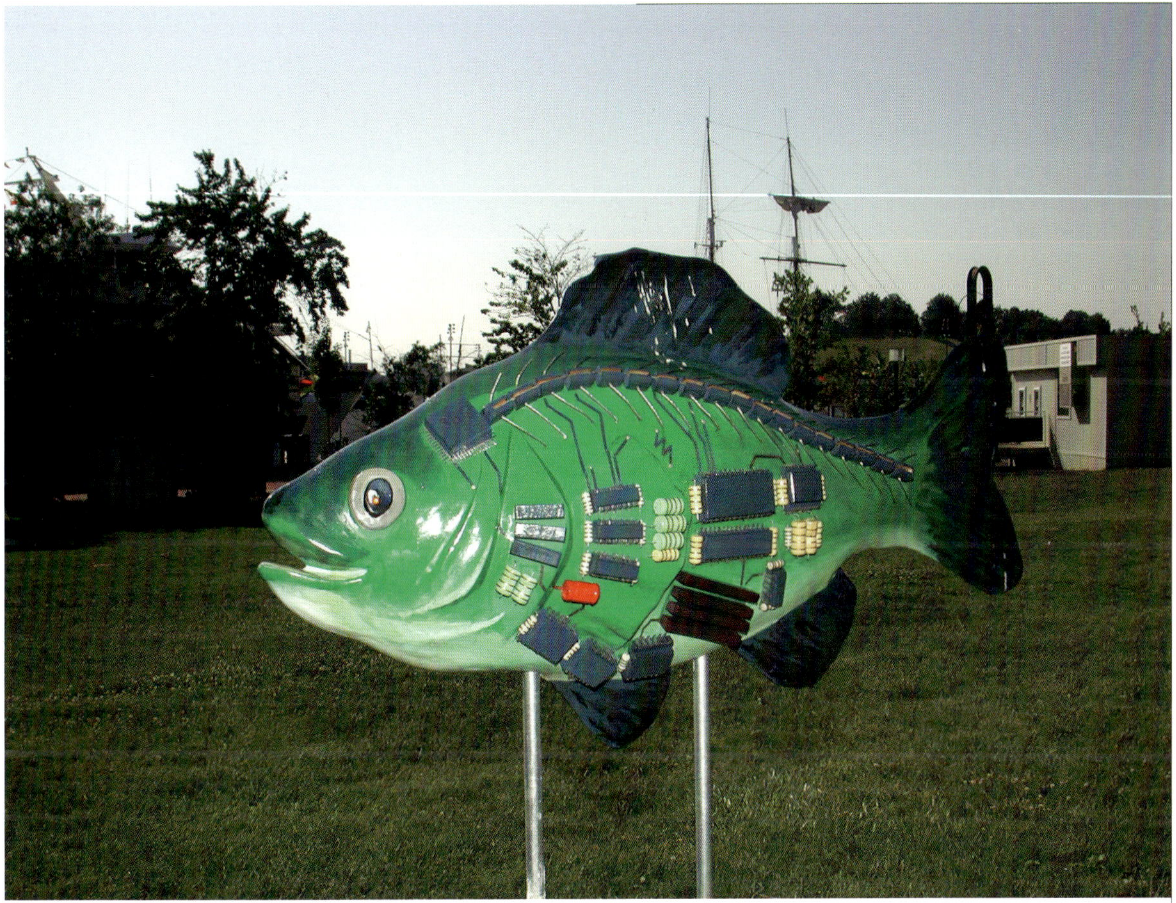

DIGITAL HARBOR FISH
David Brosch
The Daily Record

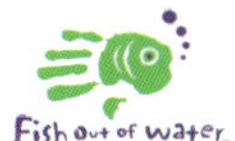

Left:

SEA-D
Mary Deacon Opasik
Struever Bros. Eccles
& Rouse, Inc.

Right :

FISHING GEAR
David Thompson
Doracon

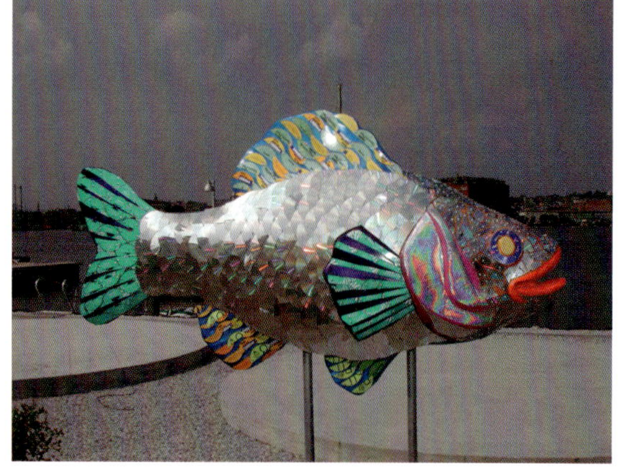

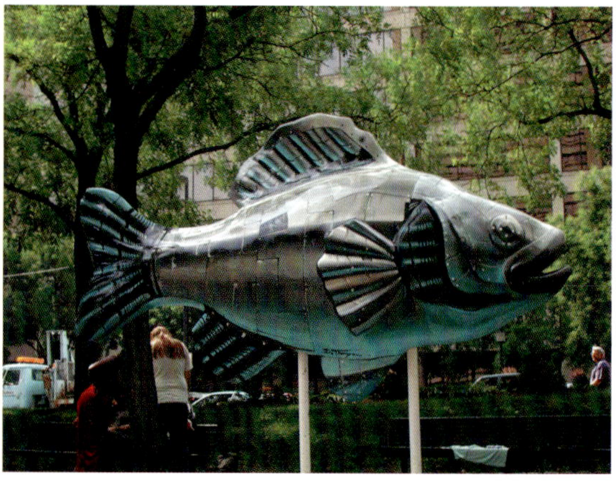

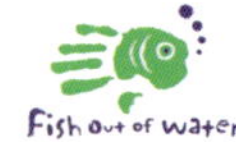

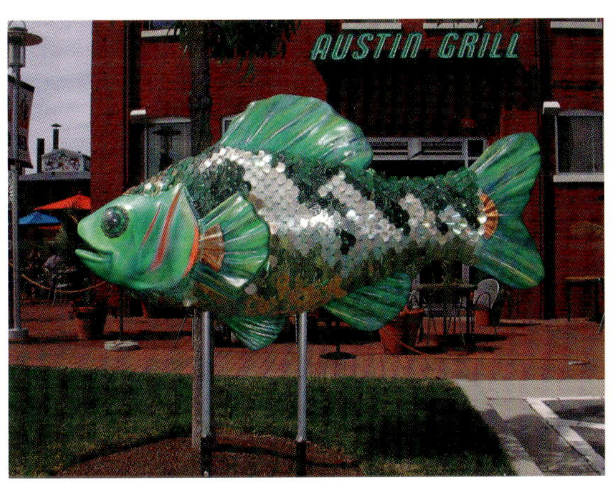

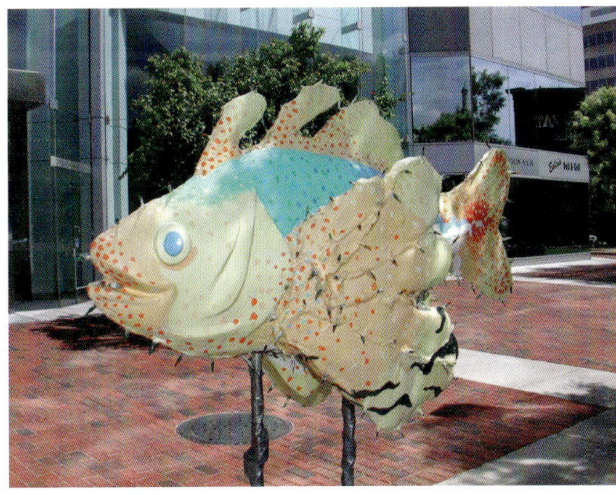

Left:

FISH 'N CHIPS
Laura Amlie
P.W. Feats / Greater Baltimore Technology Council

Right:

ELECTRIC LION FISH
Stuart Keefer
TrizecHahn

NAVIGATING CONSTELLATION 2001
M. Teresa Camacho-Hull
Audio Toys, Inc.

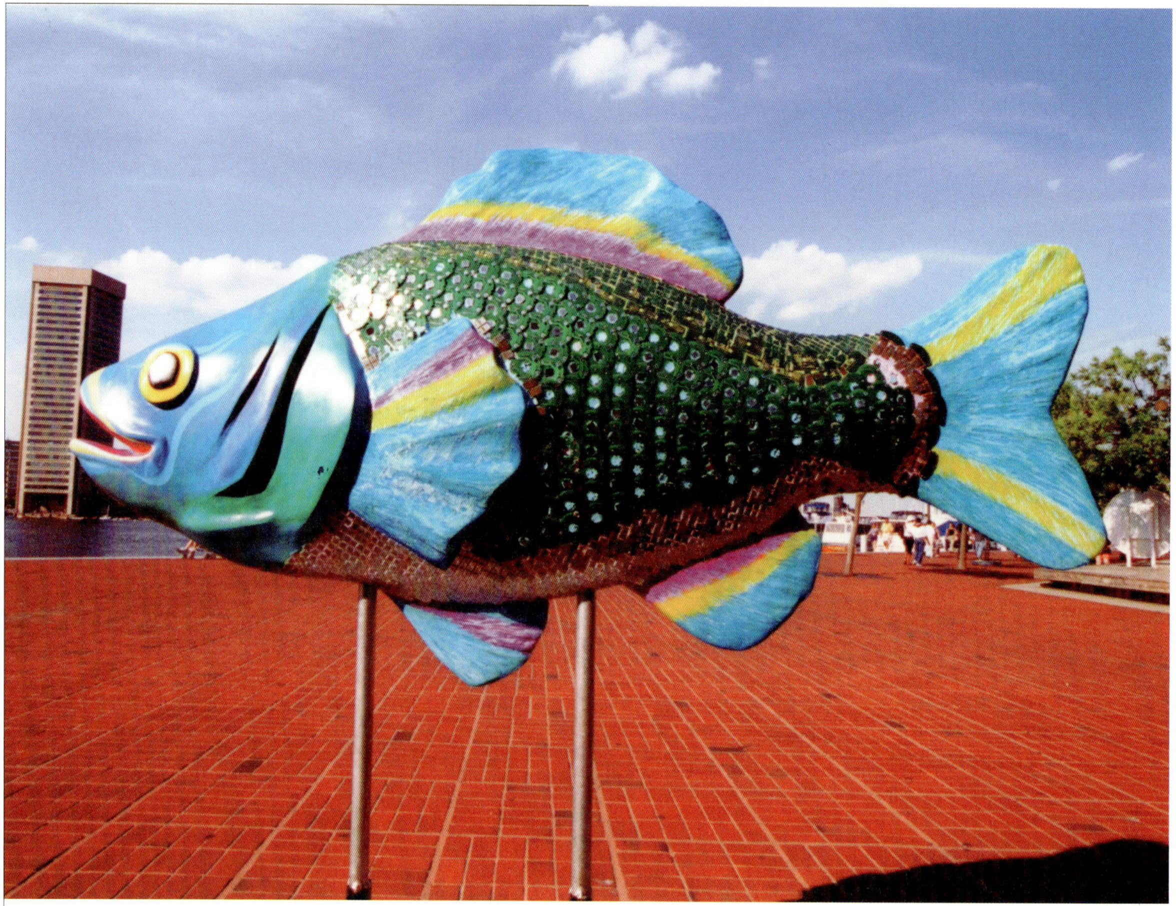

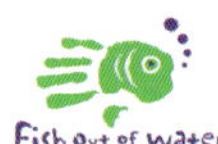

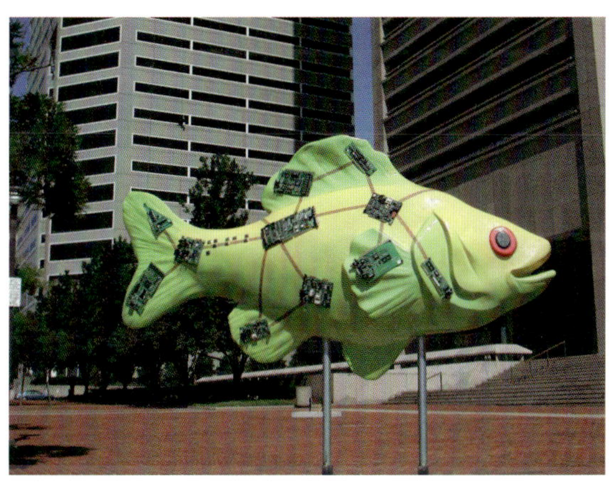

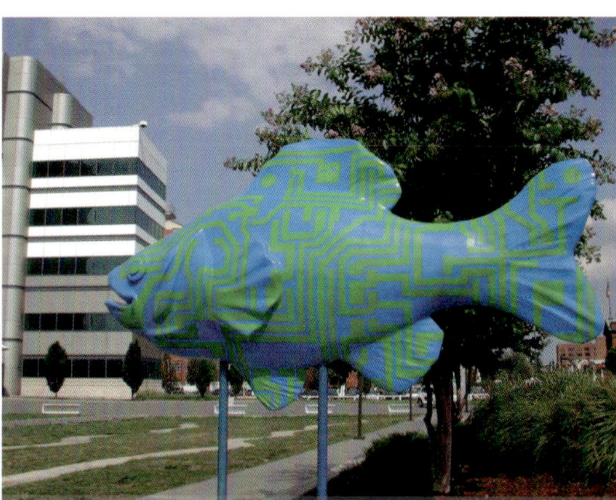

Left:

FISH 'N CHIPS

John Bledsoe and Ted Weitzman

National Federation of the Blind

Right:

MACROWAVE

Frank Perrelli

Annie E. Casey Foundation for the children and families in East Baltimore

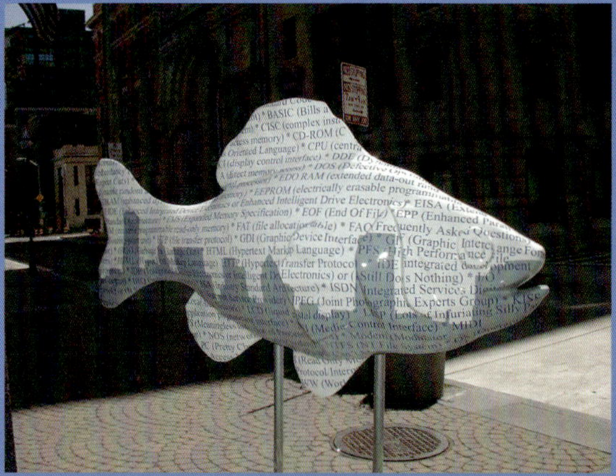

FISH & CHIPS

Christopher Hirsch

RTKL and GableSigns & Graphics

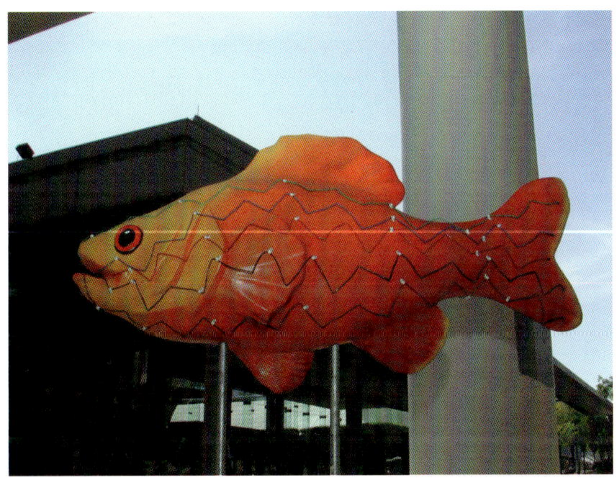

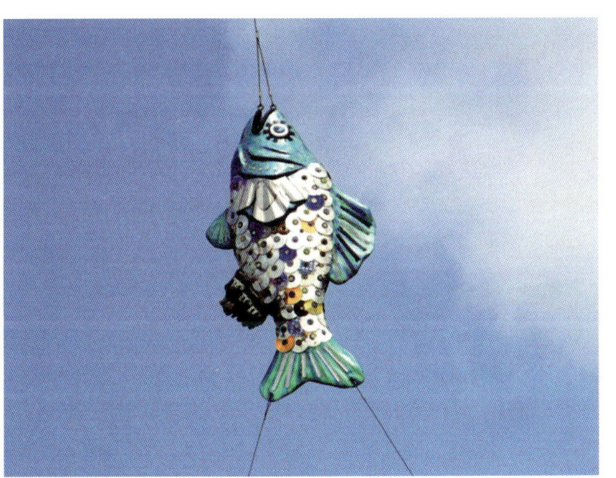

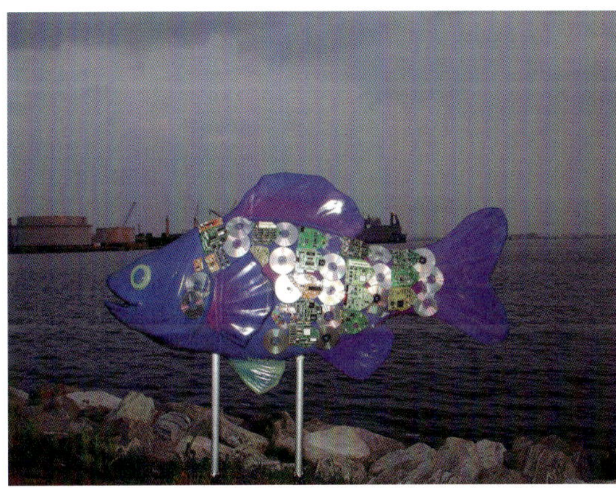

Clockwise, from top left:

FISHIN' THE NET
Access Art
SunSpot.net

HOOKED ON TECHNOLOGY
Laurie Levitt & Connie Matricardi
Greater Baltimore Alliance and Greater Baltimore Cultural Alliance

SWIMMING WITH TECHNOLOGY
John X. O' Boyle
Fish Out of Water

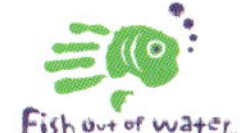

FISH AT PLAY

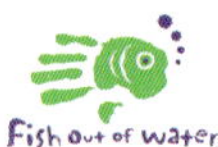

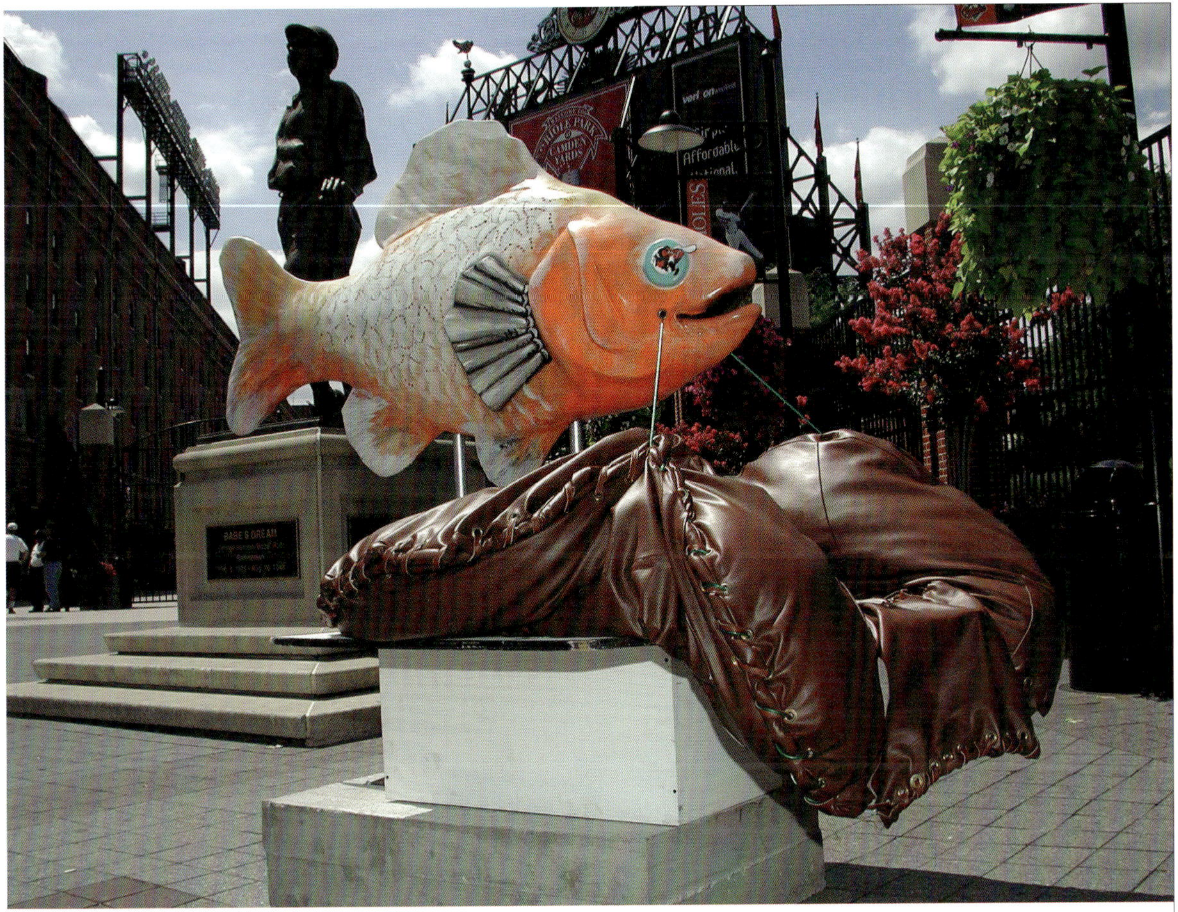

CATCH OF THE DAY

Jo Israelson & Shawn McRaney

The Baltimore Orioles

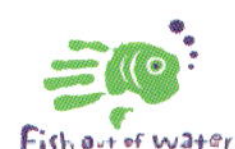

ERIC THE RED

Elisabet Stacy-Hurley

The Baltimore Ravens

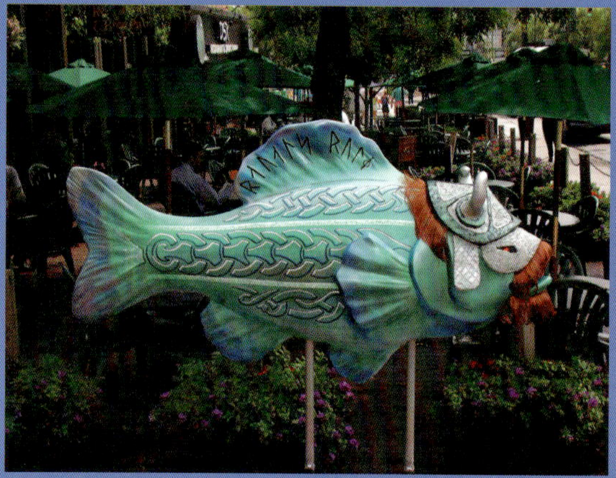

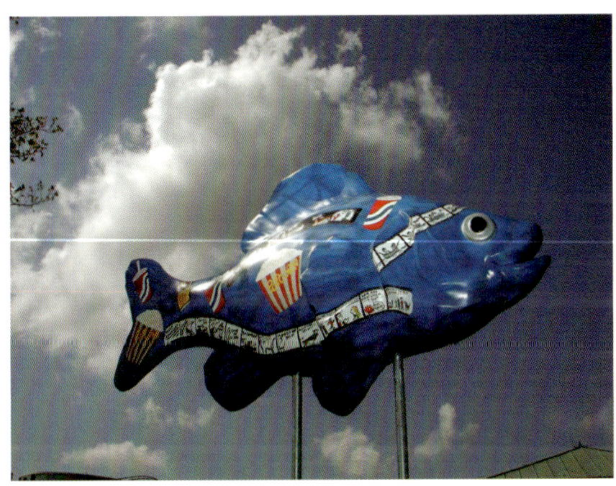

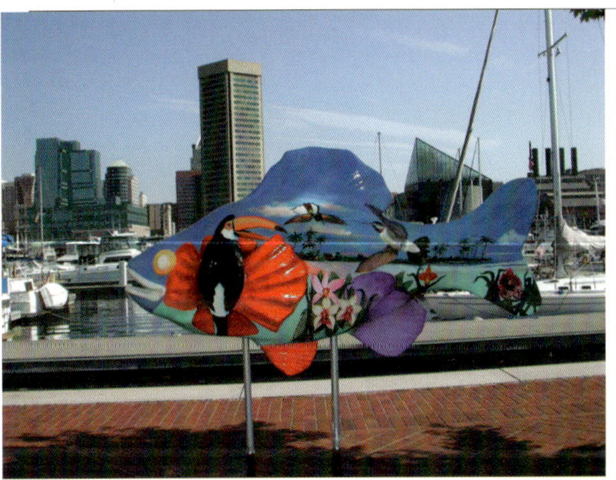

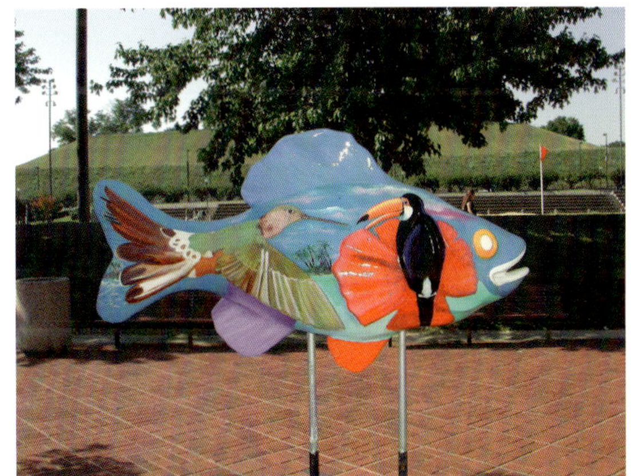

Top left:

MOVIE TIME REFISHMENT
Nina Rutledge
Pepsi-Cola

Top and bottom right:

TROPICAL FISH
Eugene R. Coles
Arlene Kaufman and Sandy Baklor

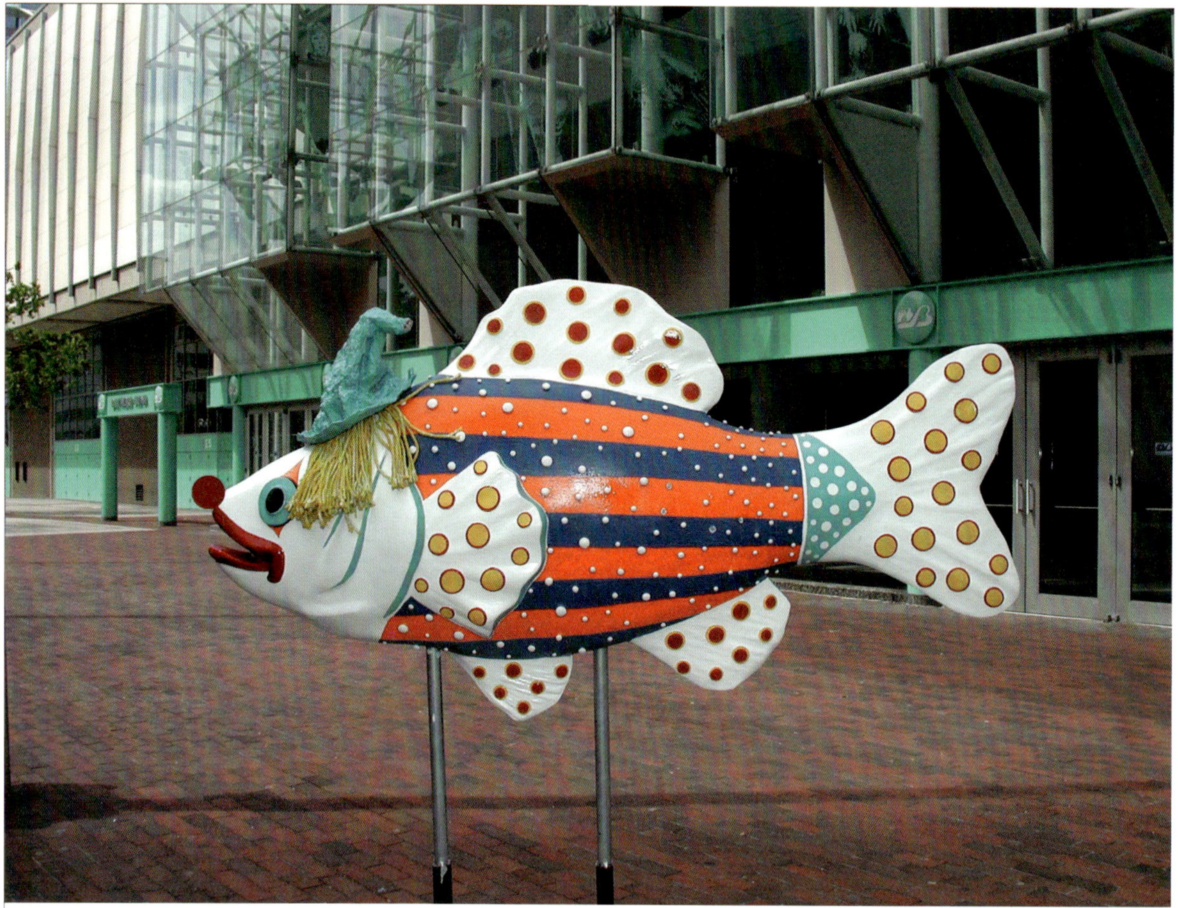

KORKY THE CLOWN FISH
Rebecca Bafford
Baltimore Arena/SMG

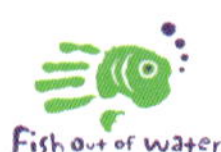

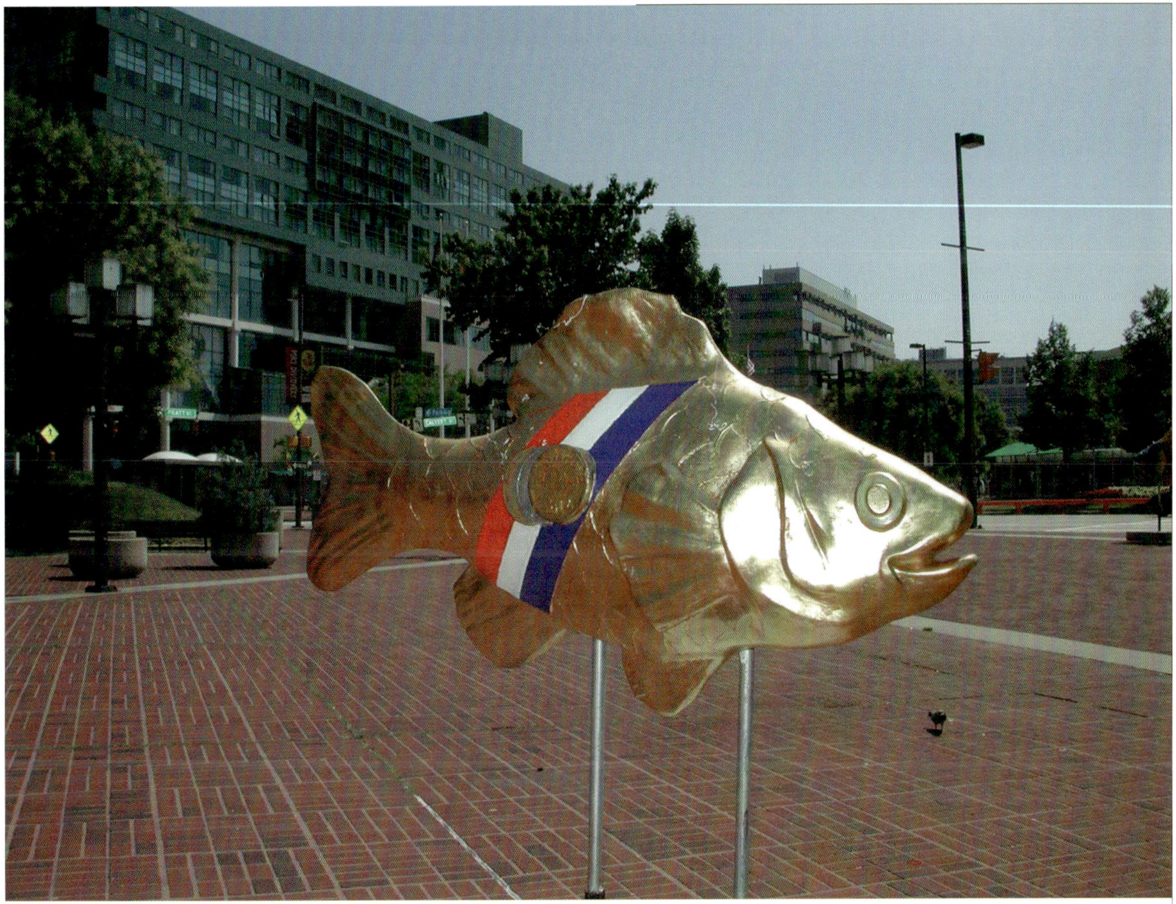

GOING FOR THE GOLDFISH

Kathleen Daywalt

A Friend of Chesapeake Region 2012 Coalition

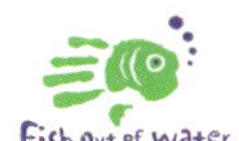

FESTIVUS (FESTI-FISH)
Tom Kelly Bauley
Baltimore Business Journal

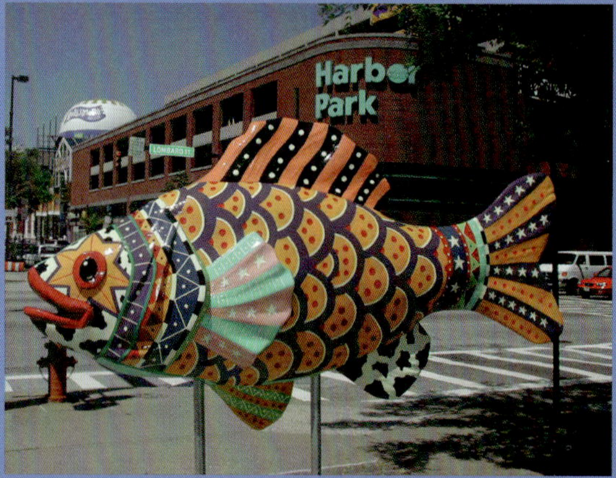

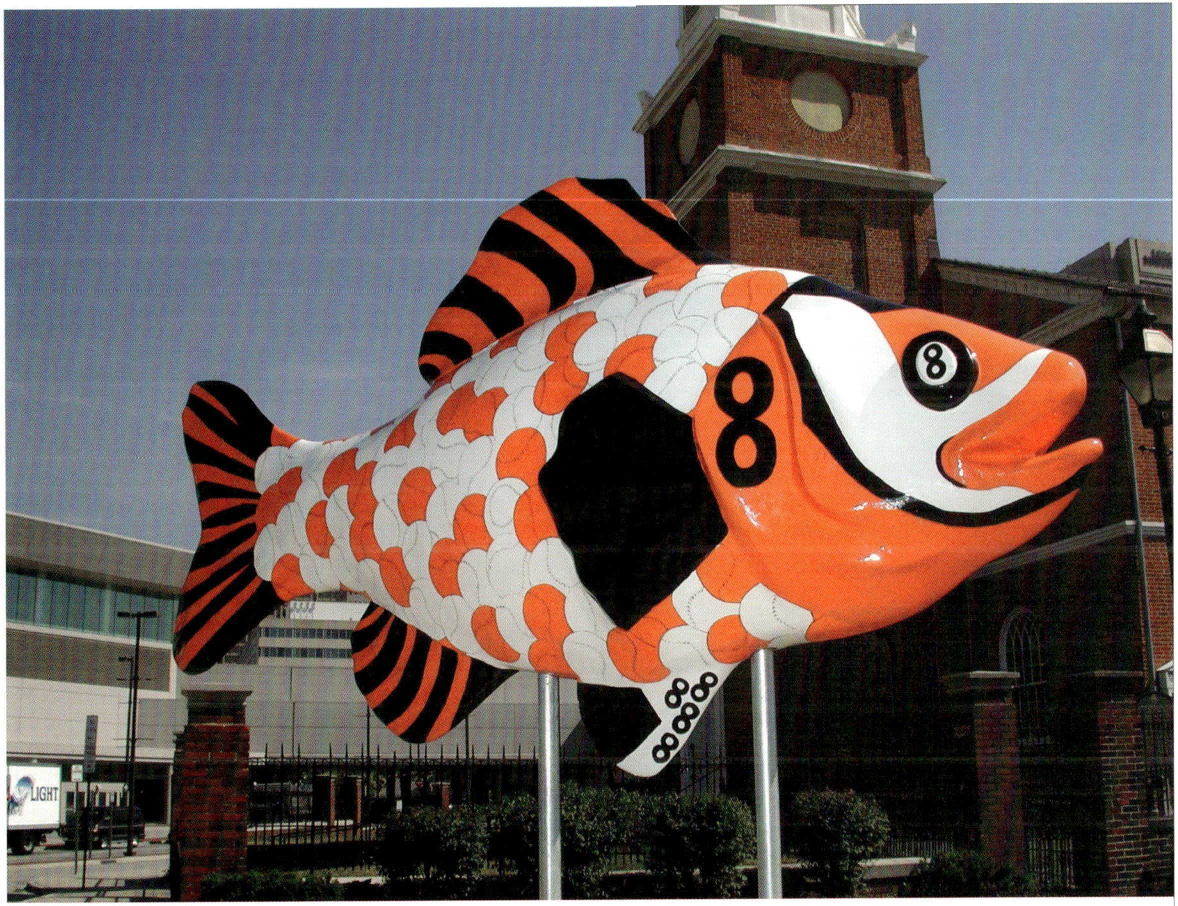

CAST IRON CAL

Yvonne Hartmann Smith

Zurich Small Business

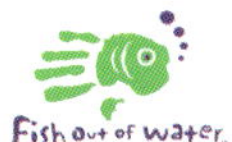

FISH IN SCHOOL

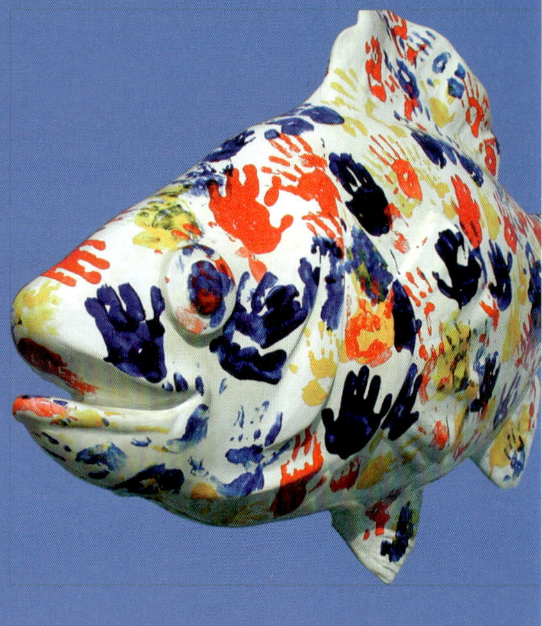

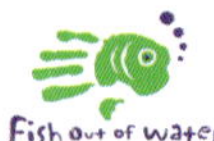

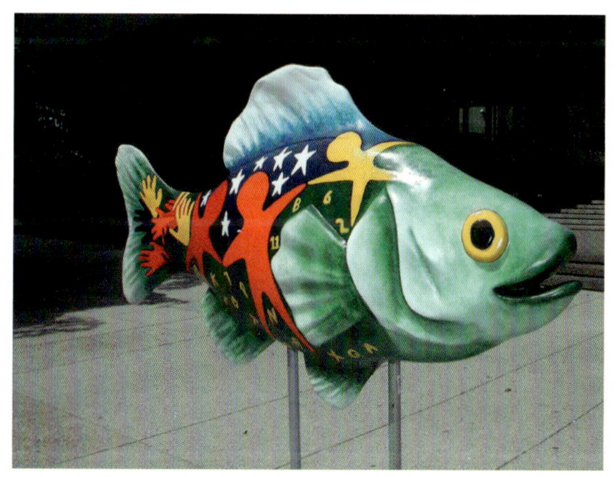

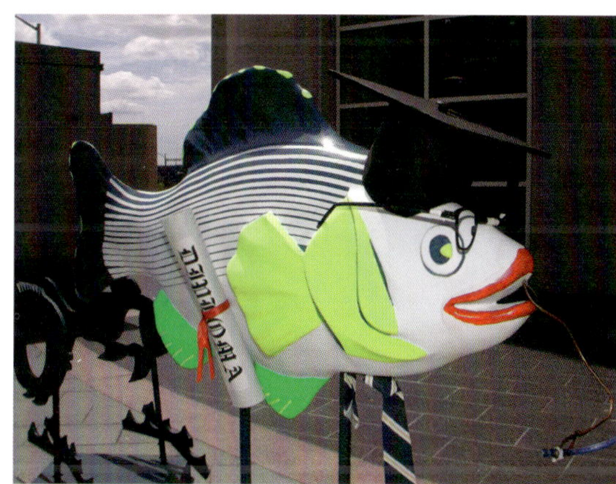

Left:

DREAMERS OF TOMORROW

Lania D'Agostino & the children of Greenmount School's eighth grade class

Venable, Baetjer and Howard, LLP

Right:

FISHING FOR THE BEST AND BRIGHTEST

Bill Donaldson, Jr.

University of Maryland at Baltimore

SCHOOL OF FISH

Susan Laugen & the students of Lake Clifton Eastern High School

Allfirst

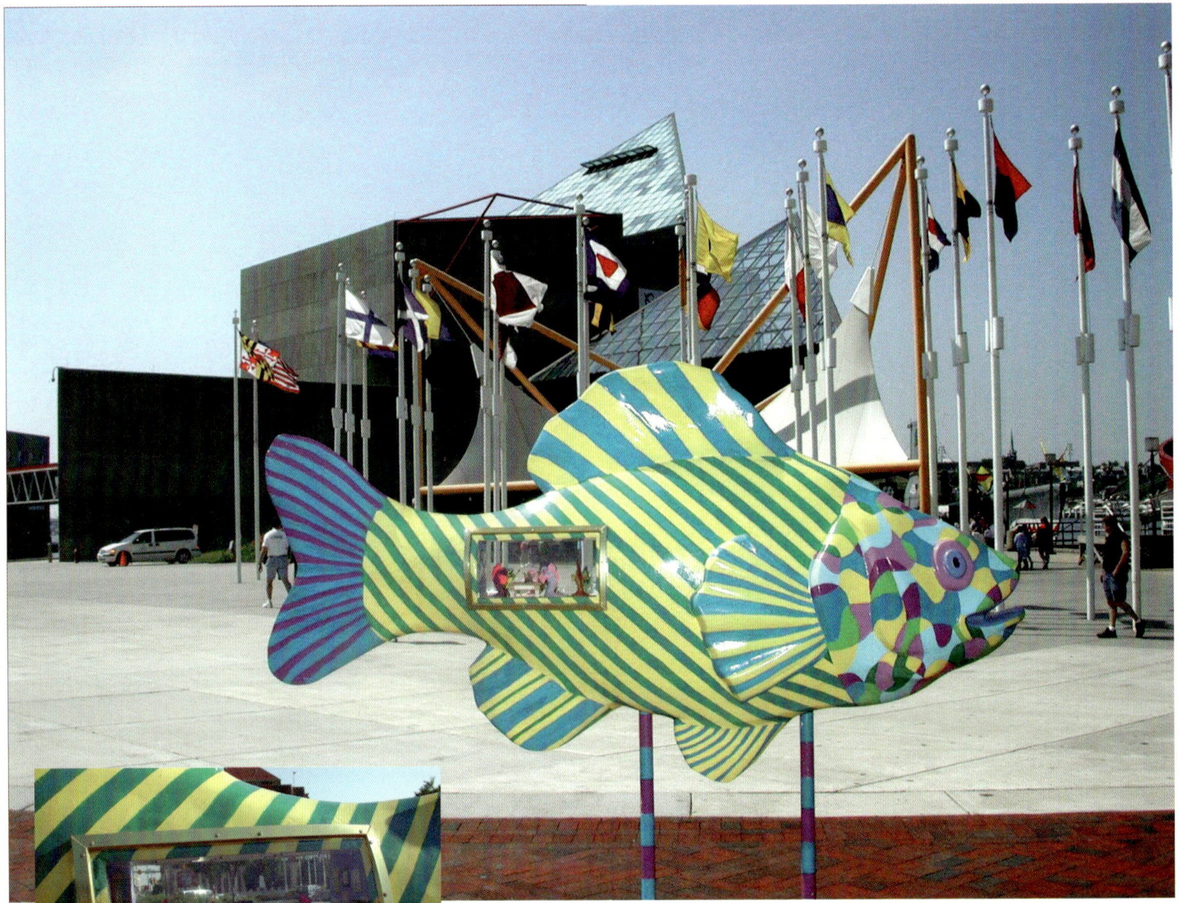

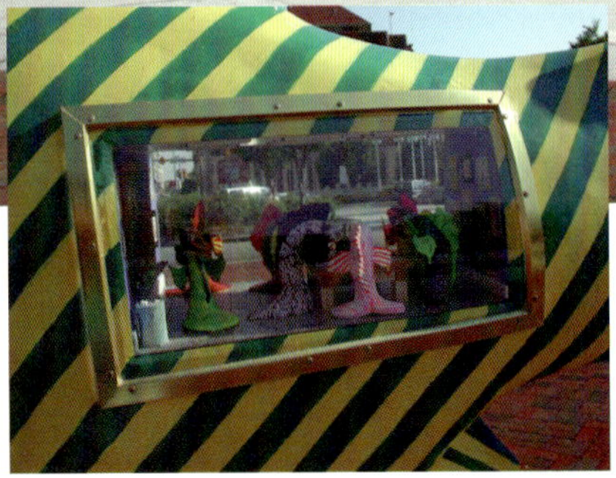

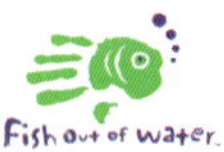

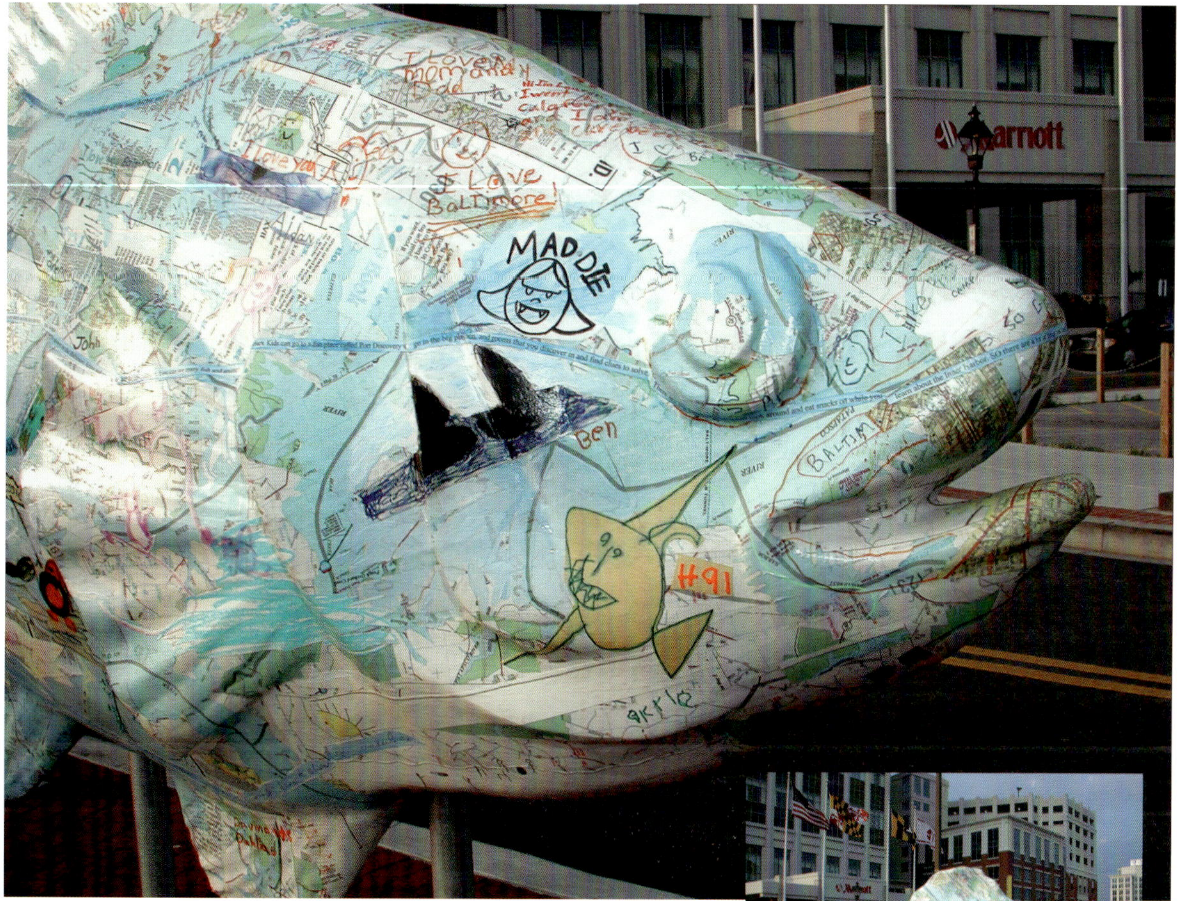

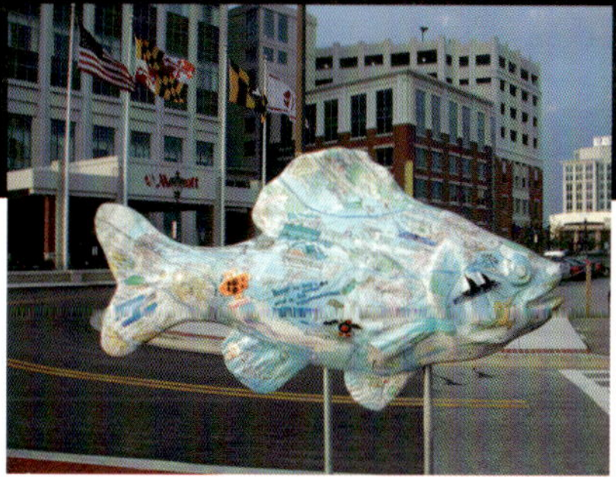

FISH FOR KNOWLEDGE

Annette Wilson Jones

Sylvan Learning Systems, Inc.

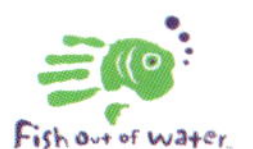

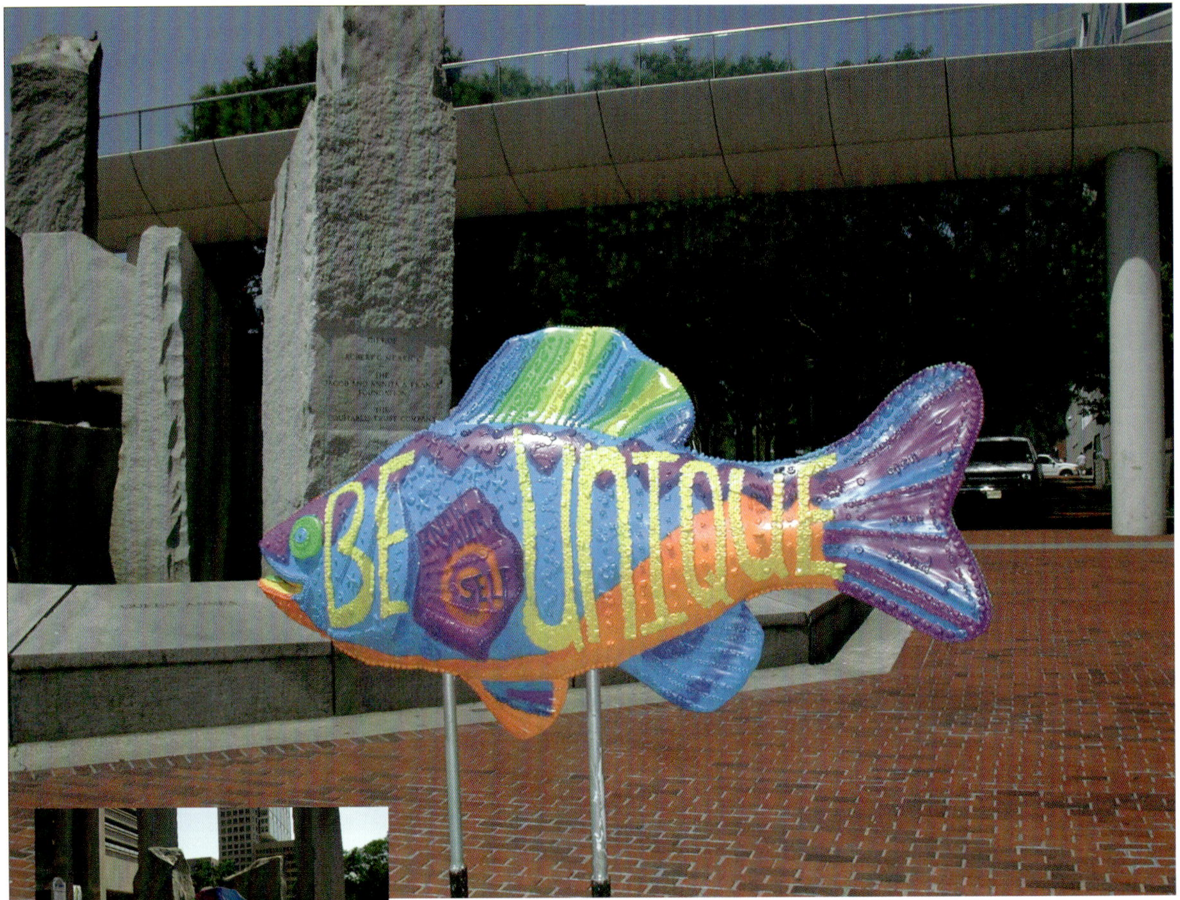

MENTOR FISH

Helen Hardesty and Megan Rowland and three students from Annette J. Brown Middle School

Ellin & Tucker Chartered

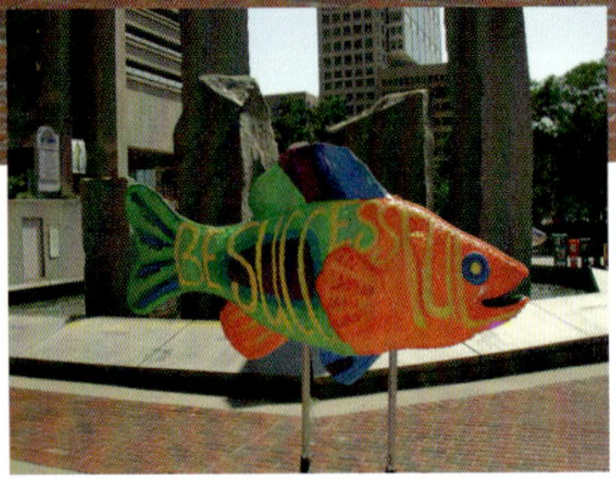

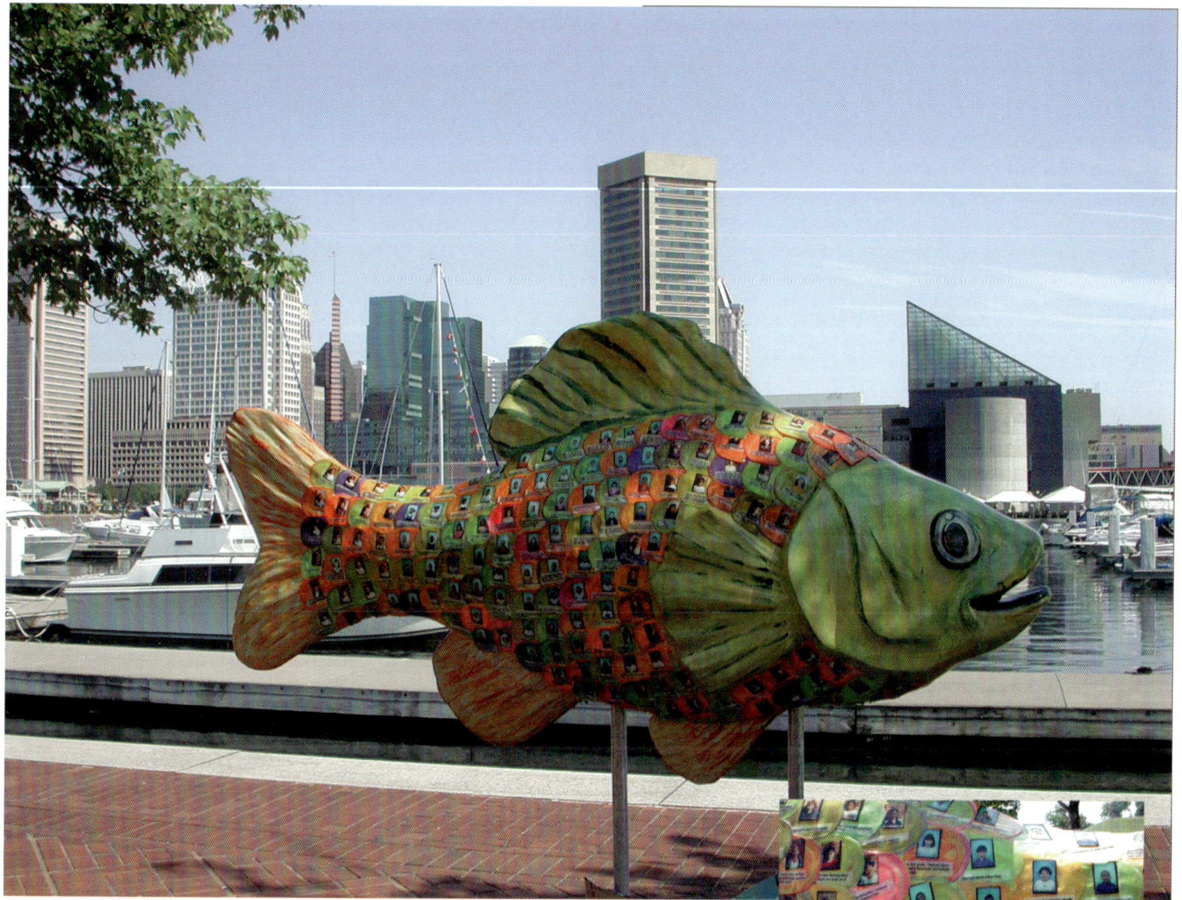

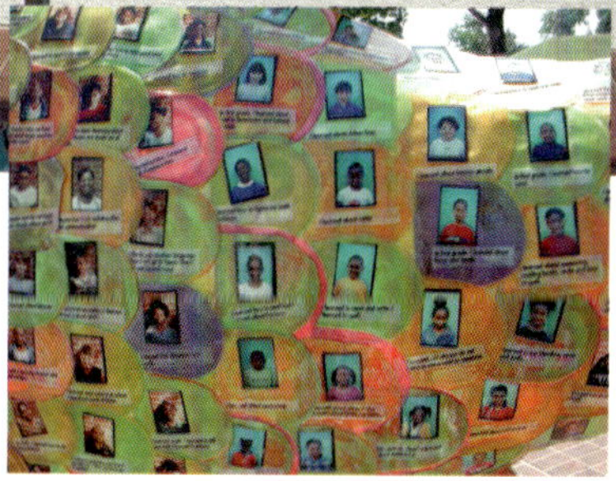

CITYSCHOOL O' FISH

Jennifer Becker & Kristine Buls

T. Rowe Price Associates Foundation

SMALL FRIES

Diane Sipple

Struever Bros. Eccles & Rouse, Inc.
for the Baltimore City school system

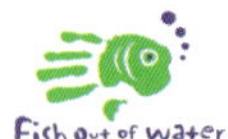

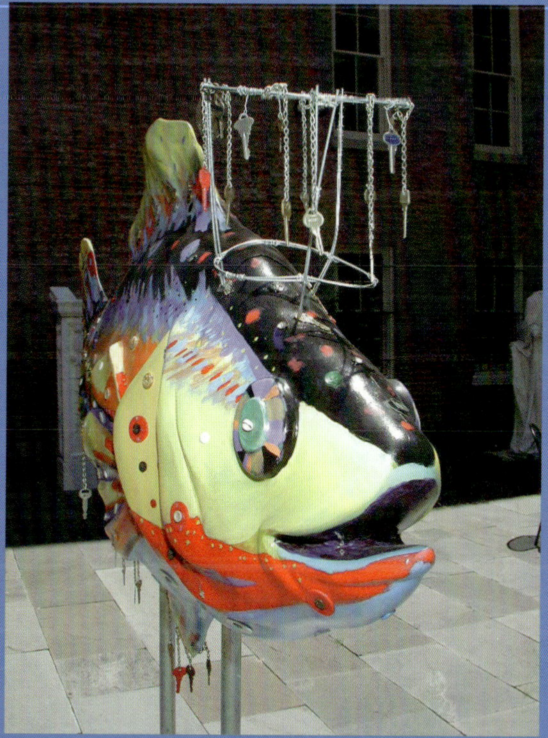

NEW DAY FISH
Schroeder Cherry
Joseph Meyerhoff Family Charitable Funds for the Maryland Historical Society

Left:

GIFT OF THE GUPPIES
Amy Elizabeth
Nottingham Properties, Inc./
The Avenue at White Marsh

Right:

TEST FISH-SCHOOLS OF FISHES
Paint Branch Montessori students/Gary Irby
CitiFinancial

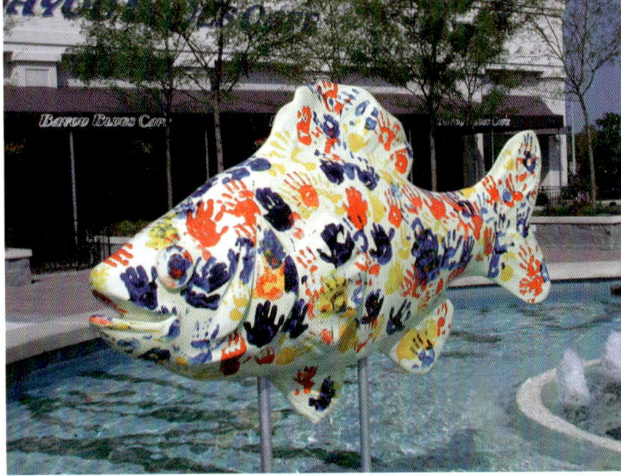

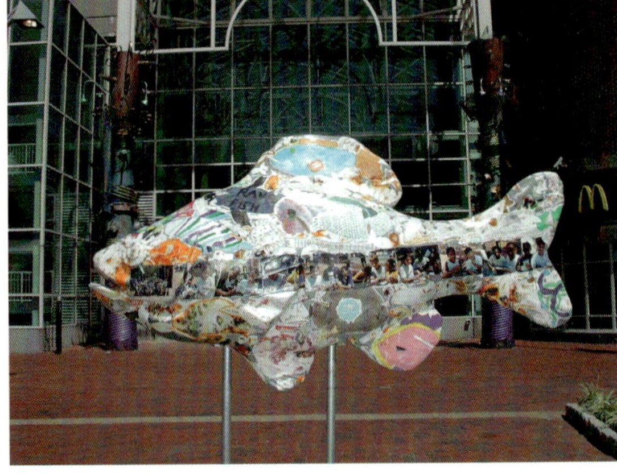

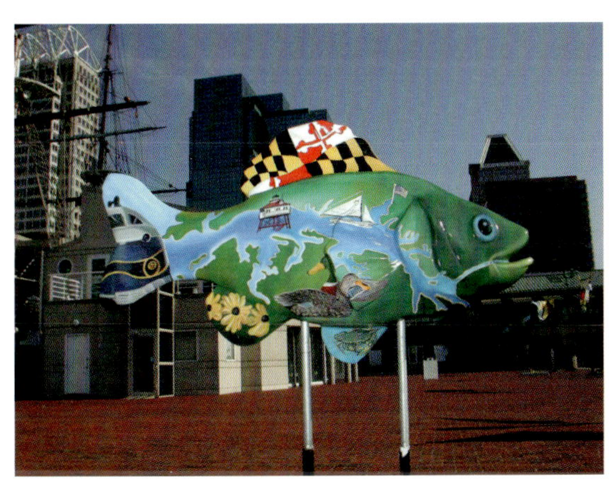

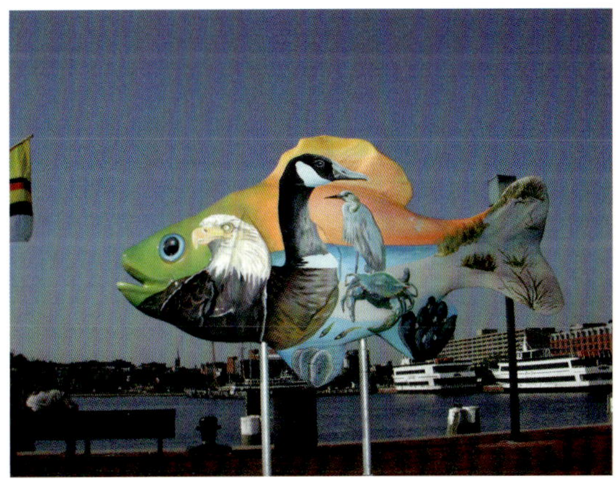

Left and right:

SCHOOL ON THE BAY

Mark W. Anthony

Chesapeake Bay Foundation
"Save the Bay"

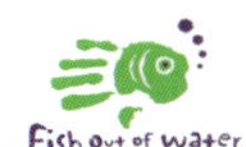

FISH ON THEIR WAY

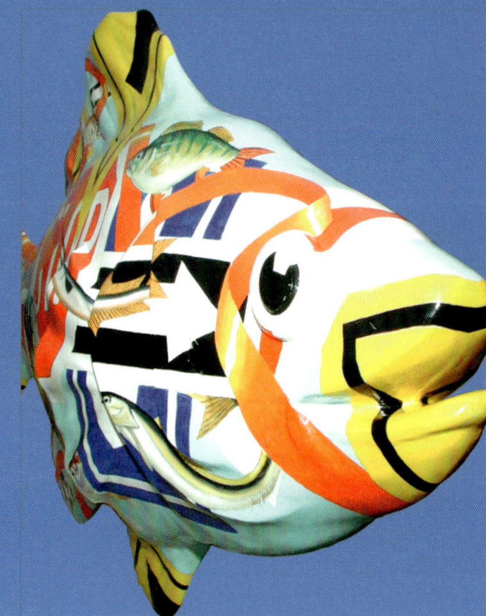

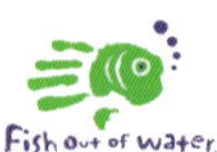

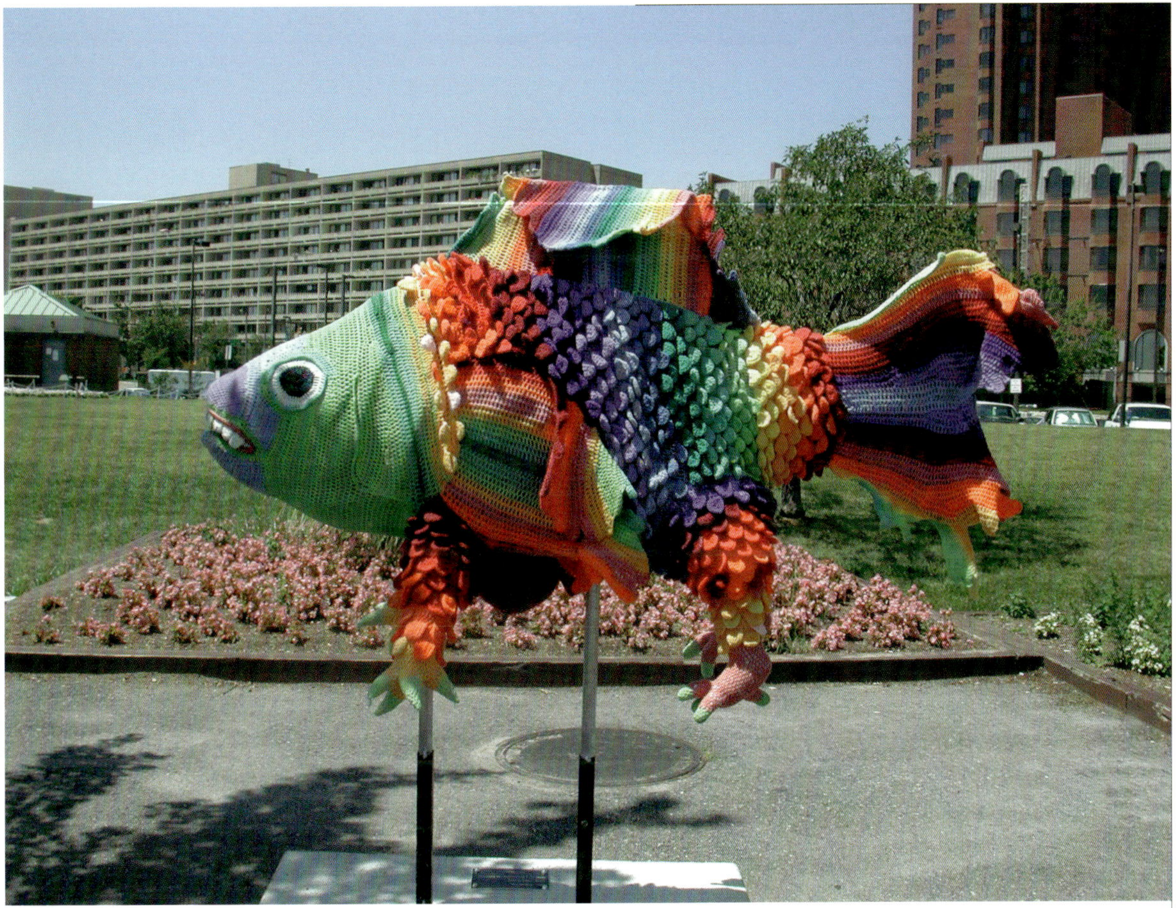

WALKING FISH
Ming-Yi Sung
Lifetimes/Patuxent Publishing

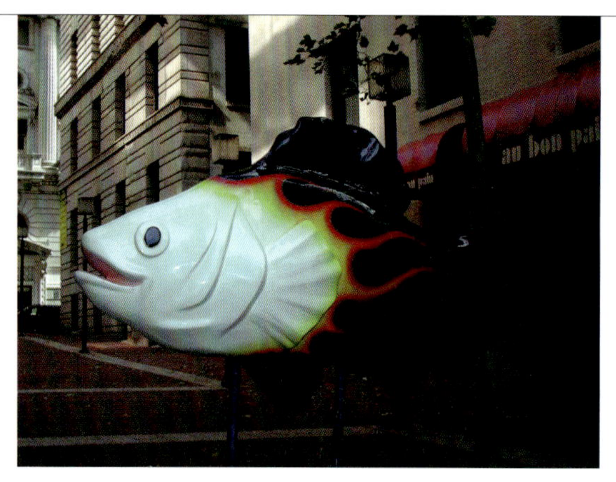

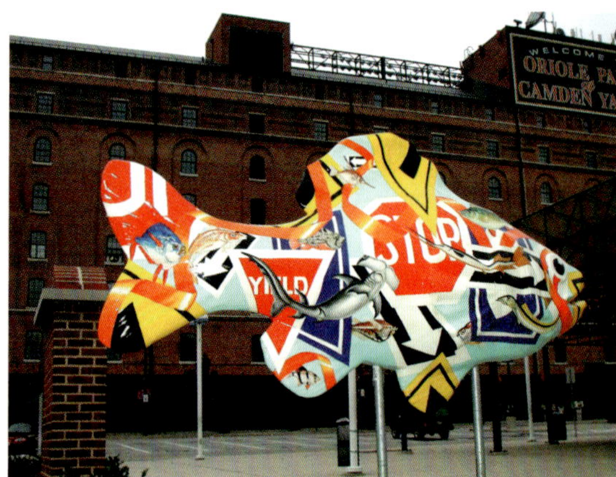

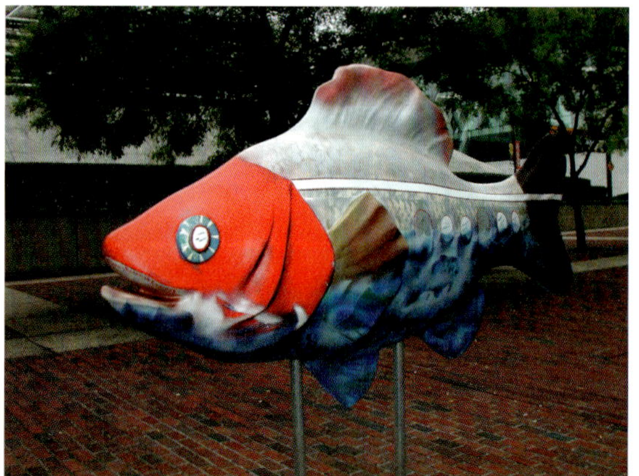

Clockwise, from top left:

HOT ROD FISH
Paul Miles
First Union Securities-Equity
Capital Market

FISH STOP
Guy Jones
Maryland Mass
Transit Administration

JONAH'S ROCKFISH EXPRESS
Arlette Jassel
United Parcel Service

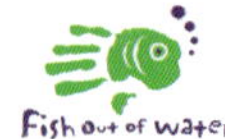

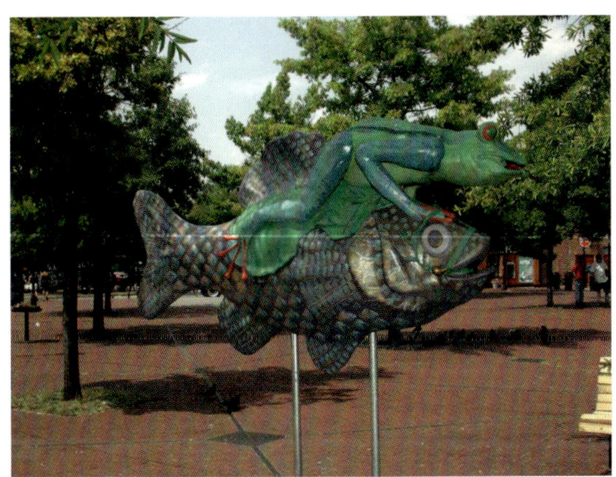

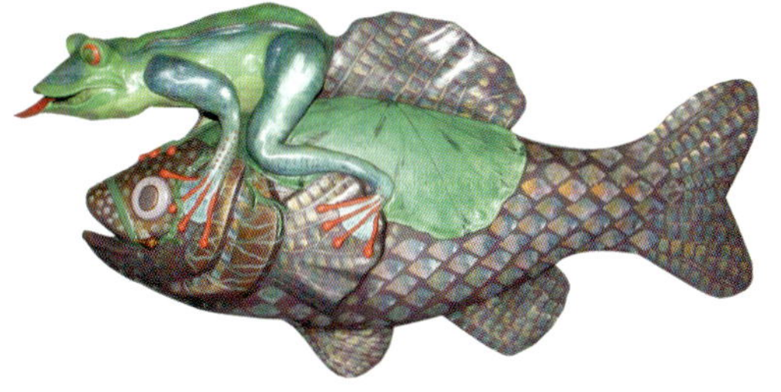

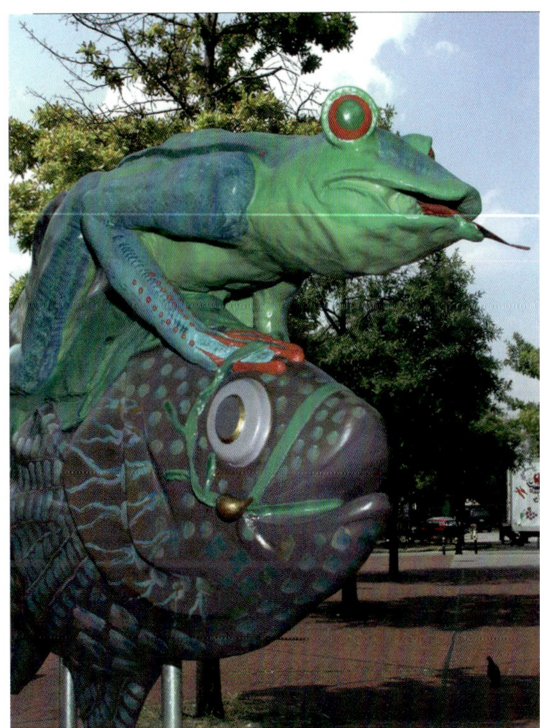

GIDDY UP
Christina Davidson & Wendi Wobbe
1st Mariner Bank

WATER TAXI

Mike W. Anthony and Sarah Barnes

Yellow Transportation

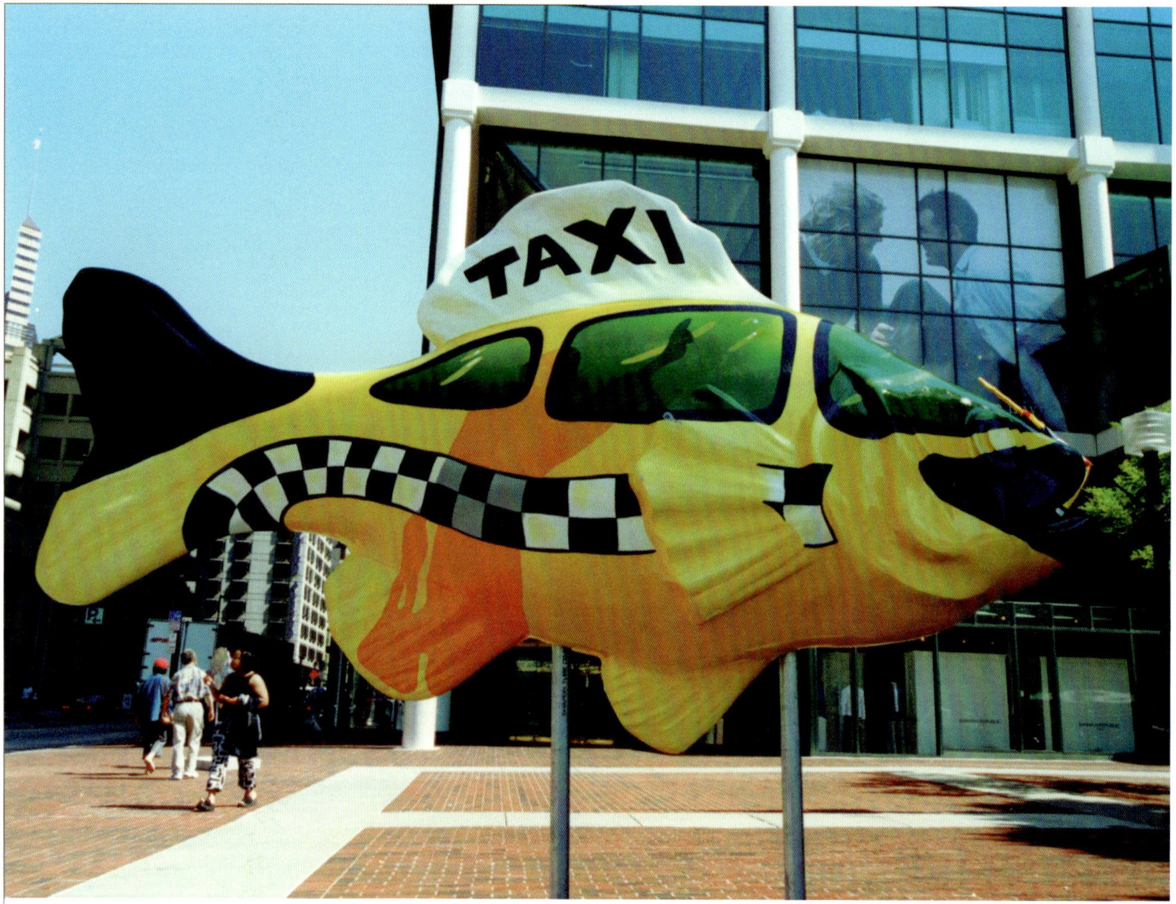

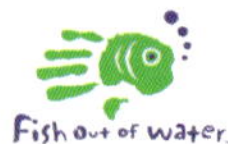

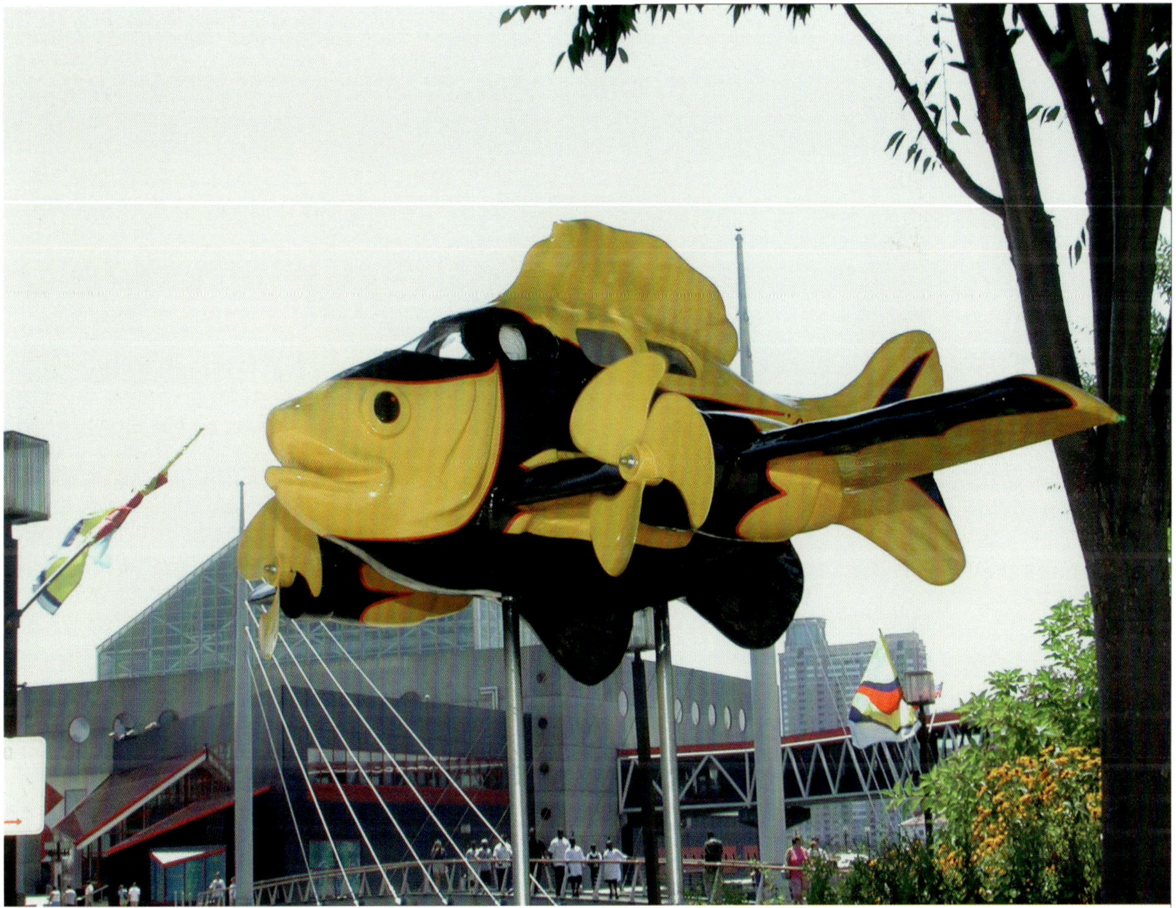

PLANE OL' FISH
Steven Weitzman
National Aquarium in Baltimore

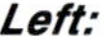

Left:

TALL FISH
George Lucas
Weinberg Harris and
Associates, Inc.

Right:

PILOT FISH
Konstantinos Damalas
Gordon, Feinblatt, Rothman,
Hoffberger & Hollander LLC

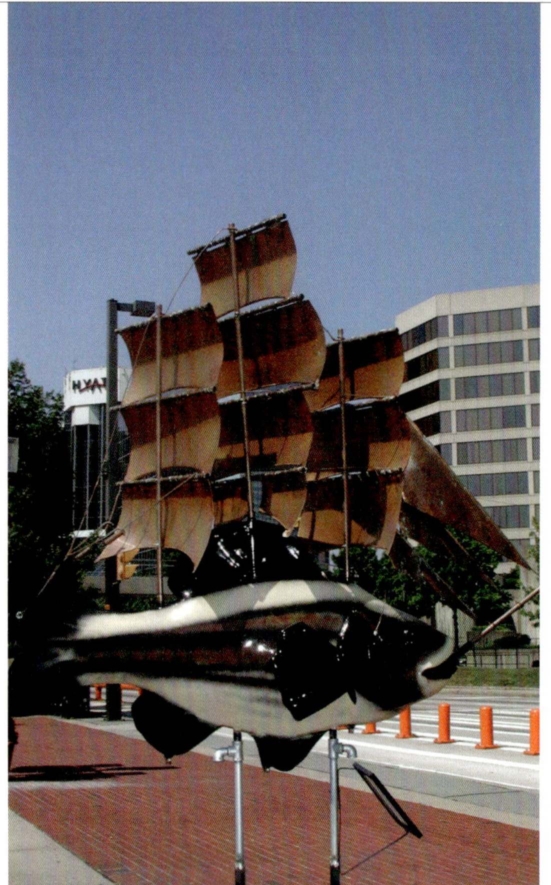

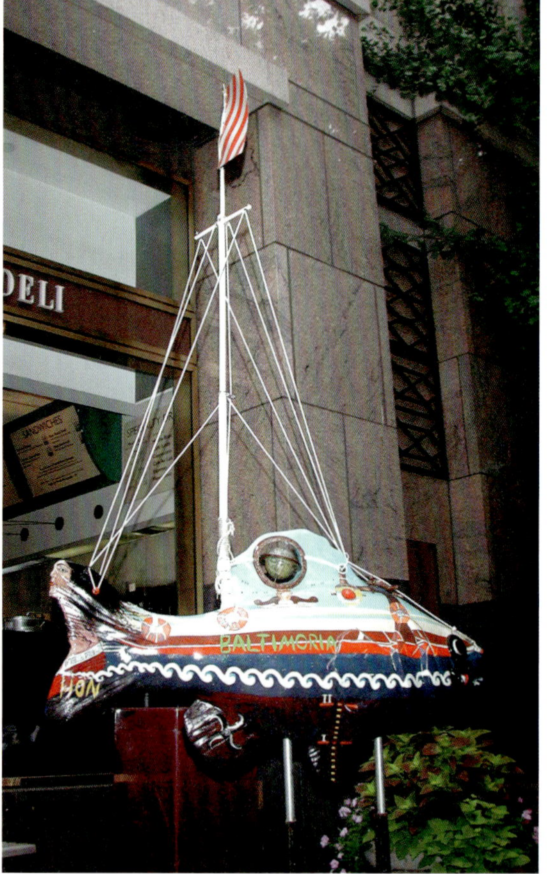

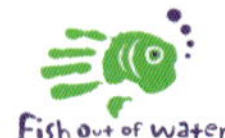

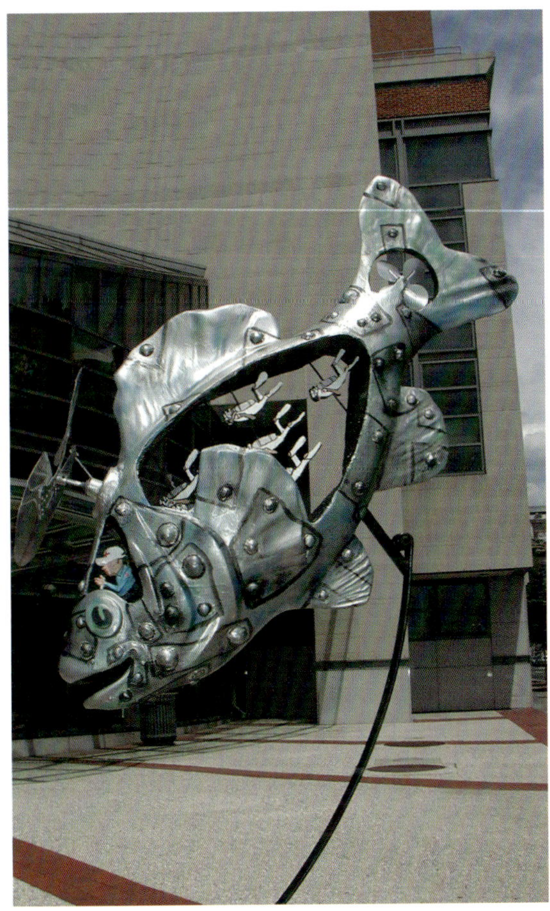

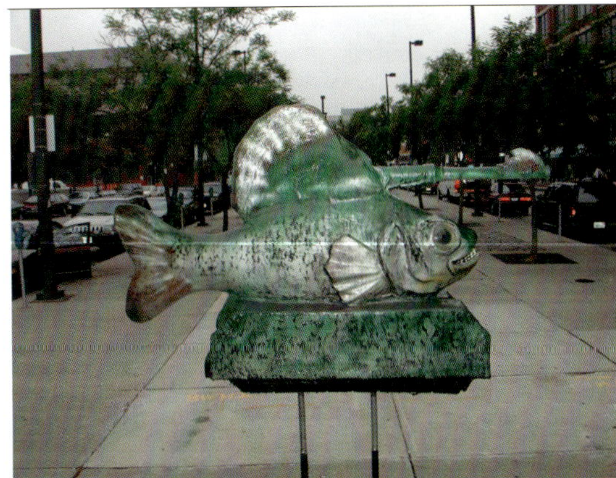

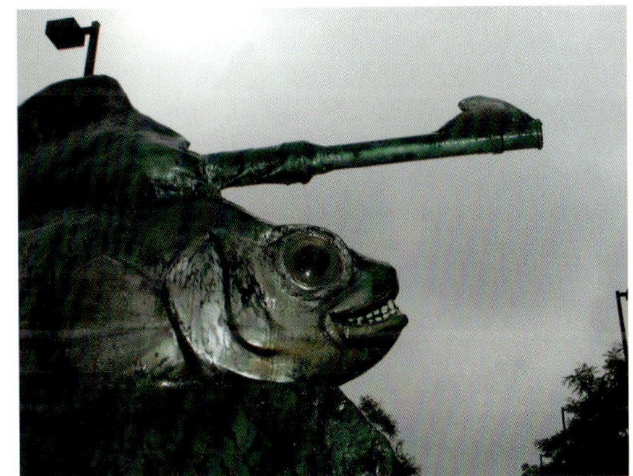

Left:

HELI-FISH
Leslie Heins
University of Maryland Medical System

Right top and bottom:

FISH TANK (NATURE FIGHTS BACK)
Steve Estes
Sierra Military Health Services, Inc.

FISH AS CHARACTERS

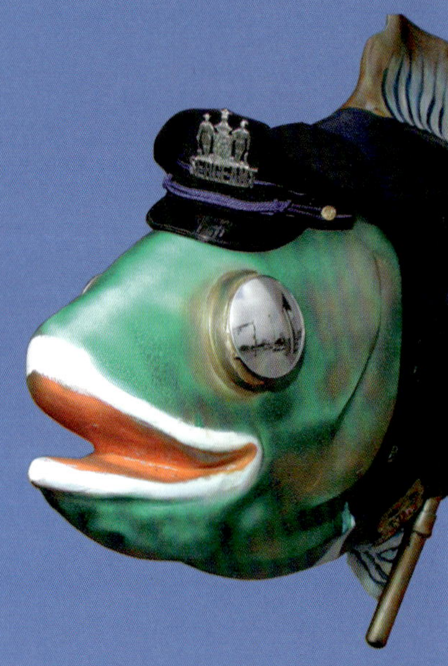

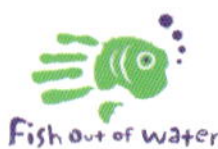

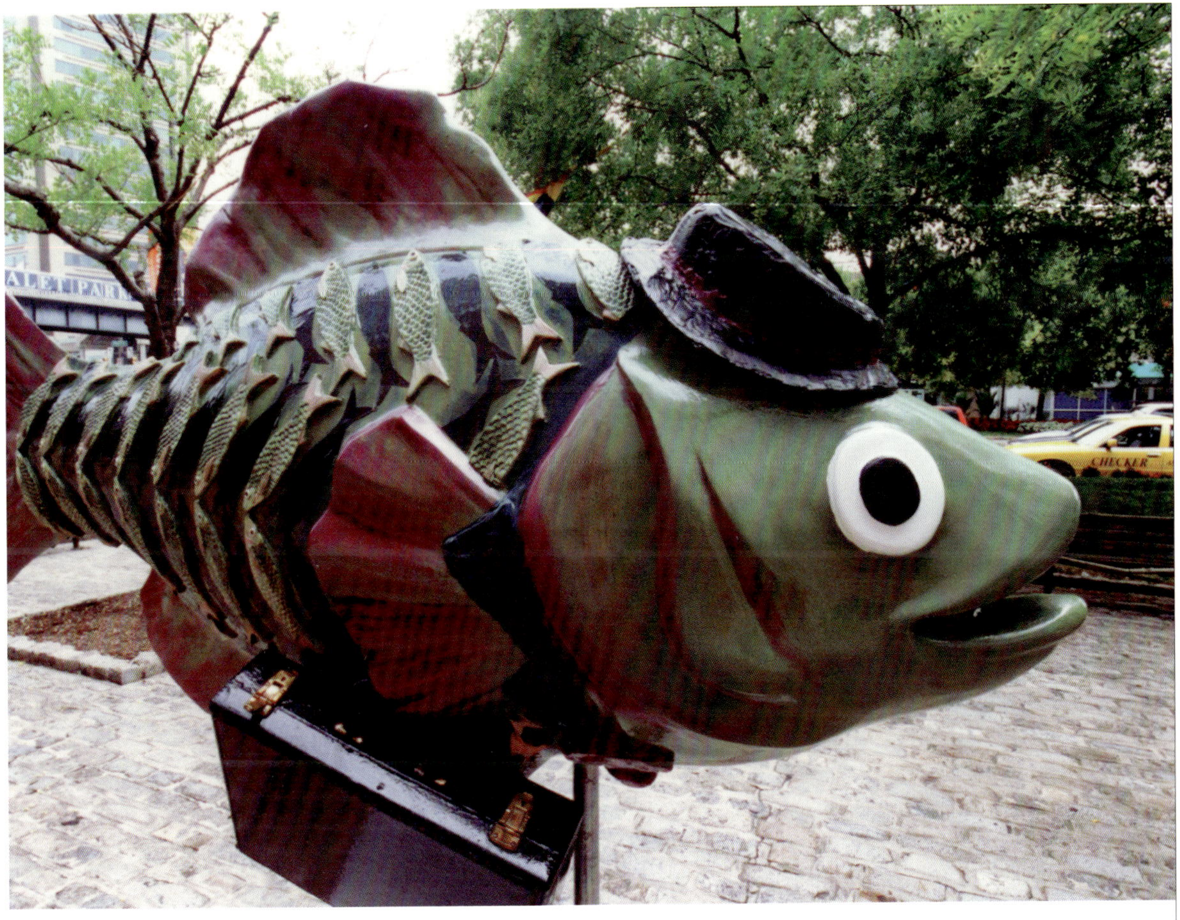

HERRING BONE SUIT
Suzanne Herbert-Forton
France-Merrick Foundation

Top left to right:

PRINCE BOGARD WITH TRIGGER
Joan Danziger
The Frank Foundation

OFFISHER FINLY
Noelle Zeltzman
Fish Out of Water

Bottom left and right:

FISHY CAMOUFLAGE
Matthew A. Gerring
Planned Parenthood of Maryland

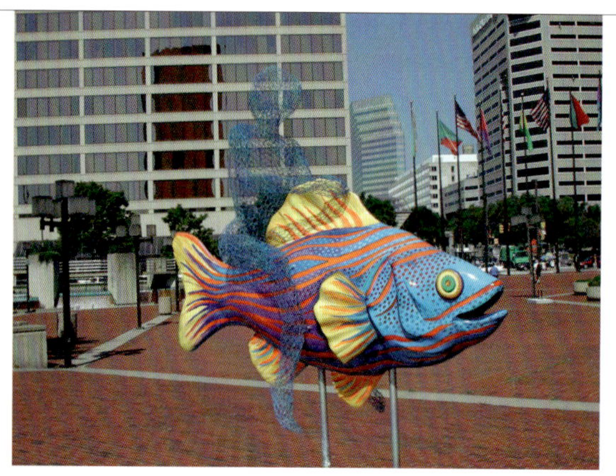

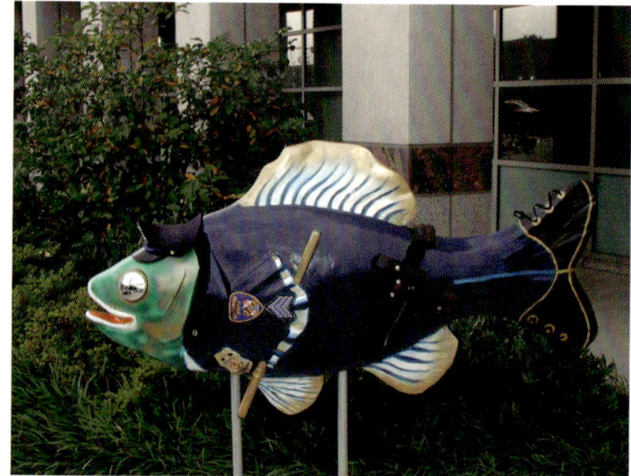

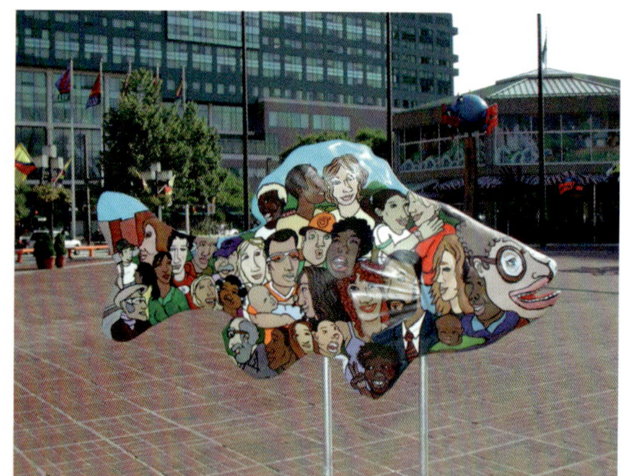

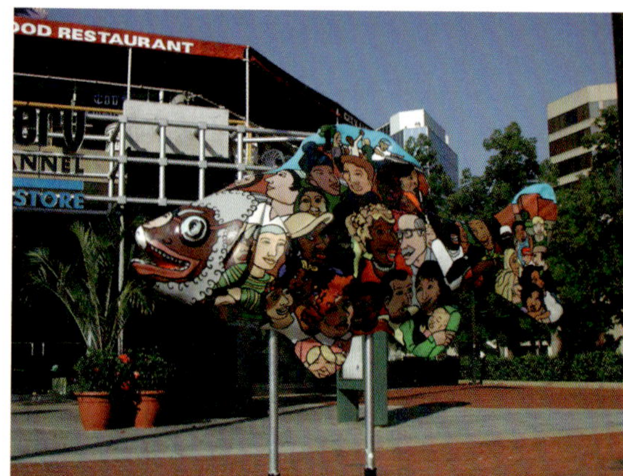

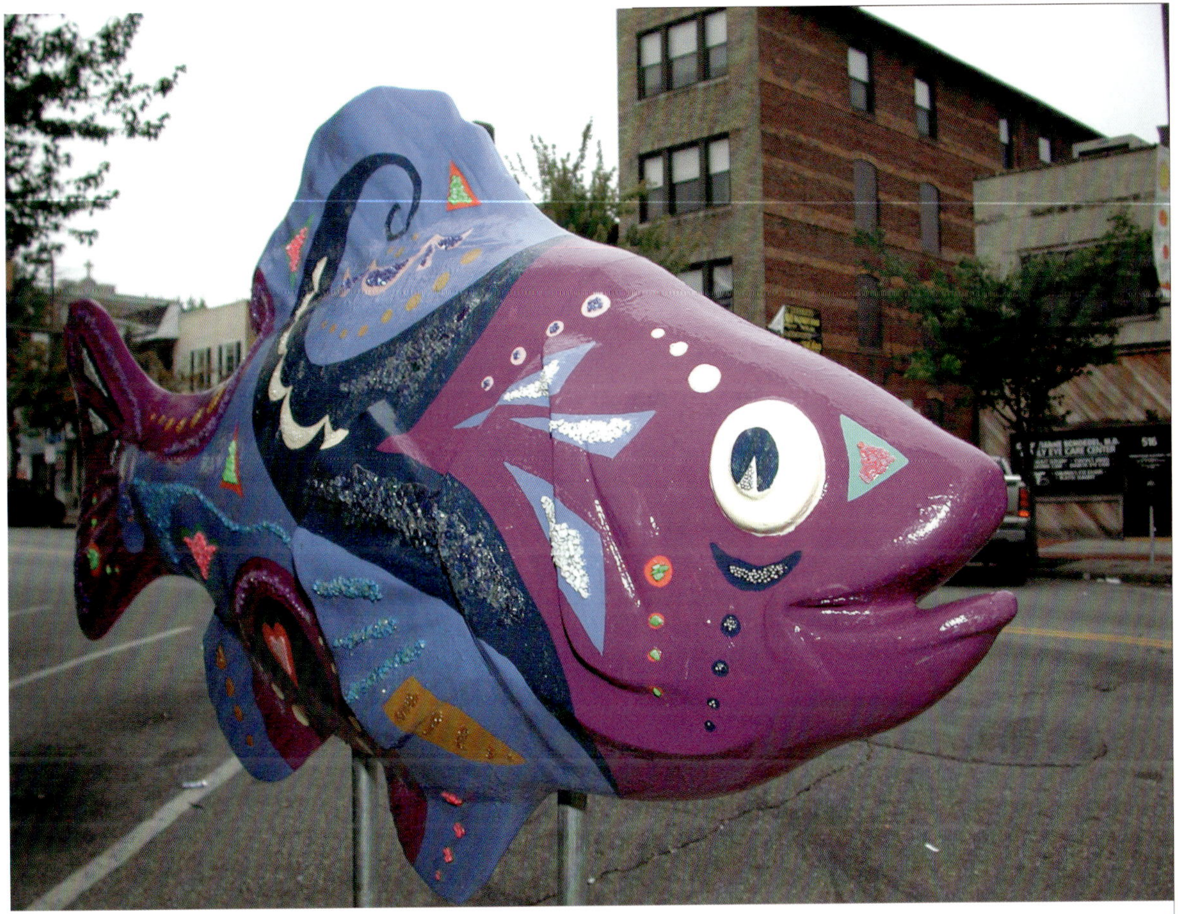

ROXY THE ROCK FISH

Tim Lonergan

Highlandtown Merchants Association

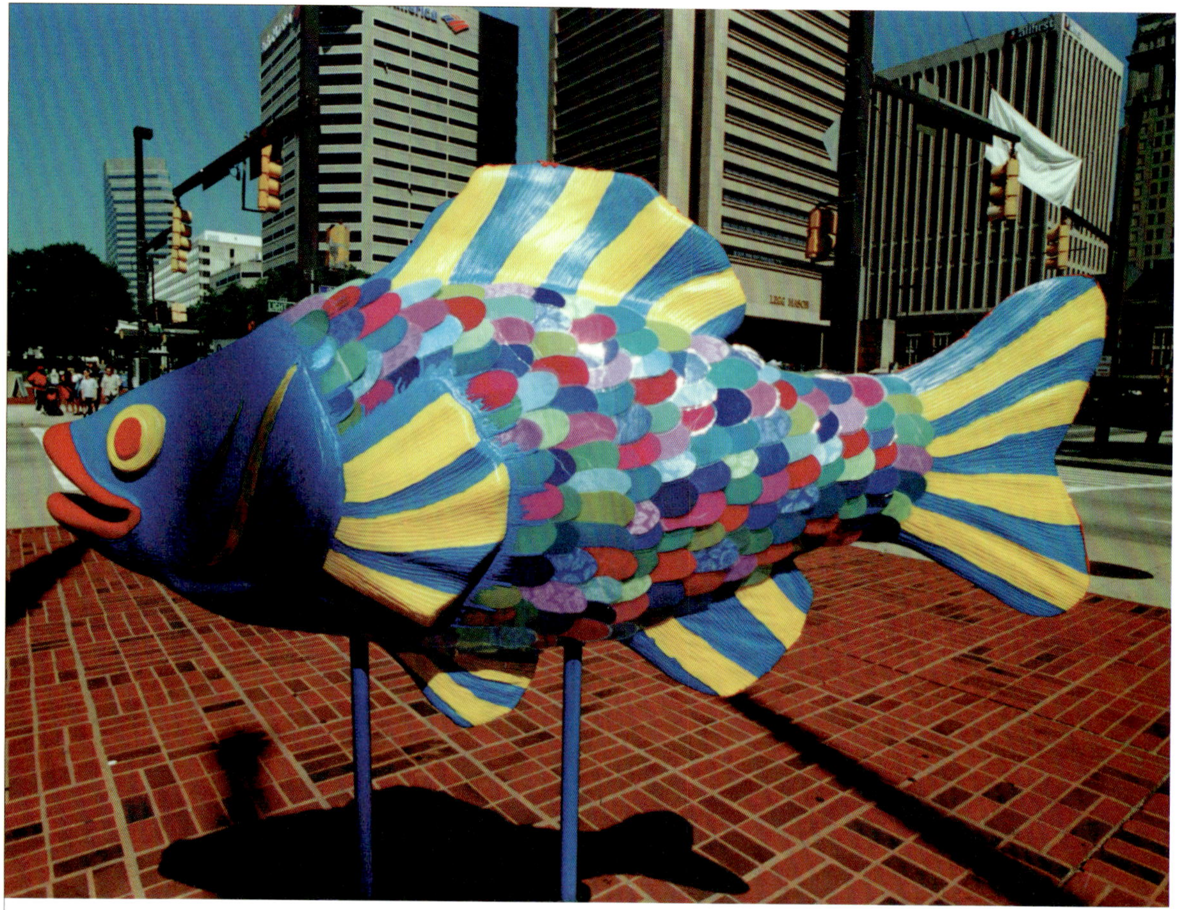

BALTI THE KISSERFISH

Christiane M. Graham

Harry and Jeanette Weinberg Foundation

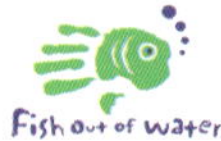

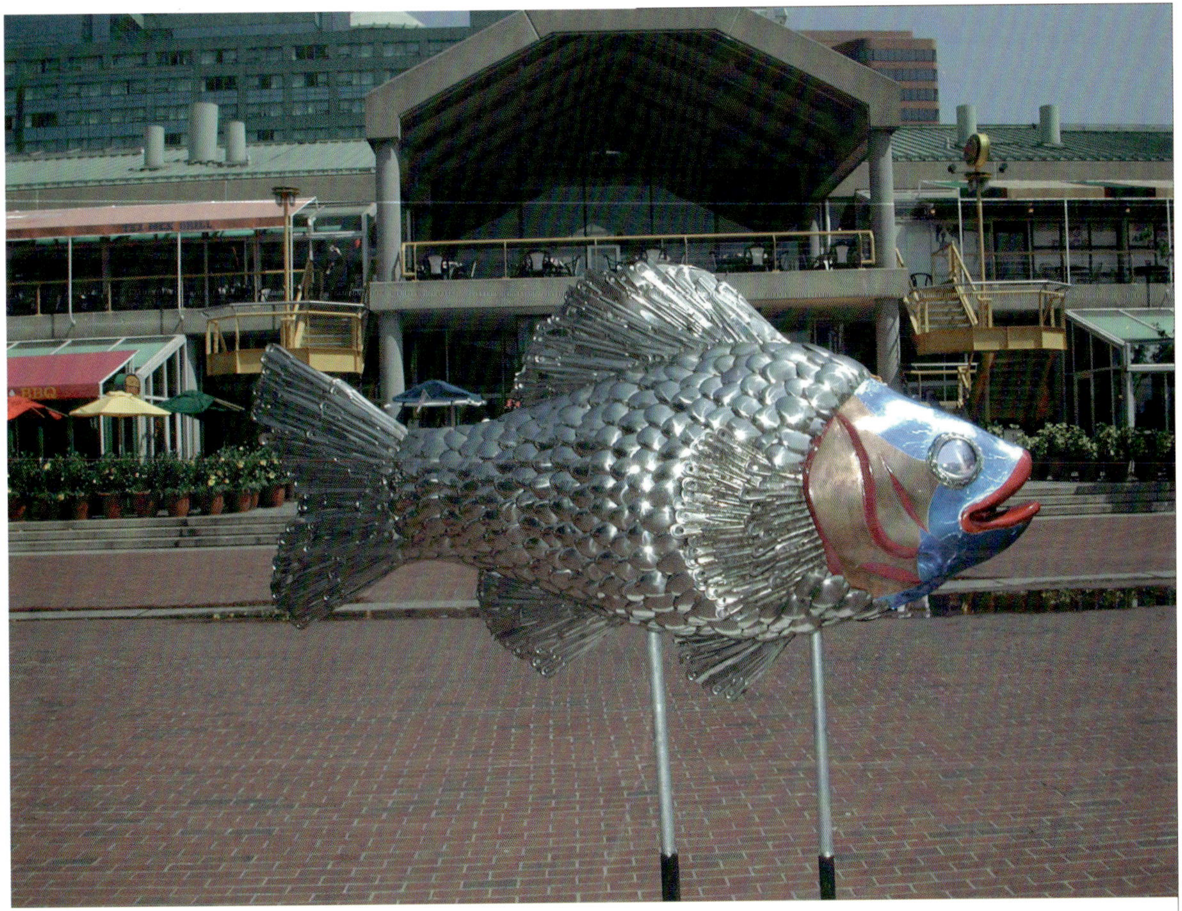

SPOON-A
Jim Opasik
Chesapeake Partners

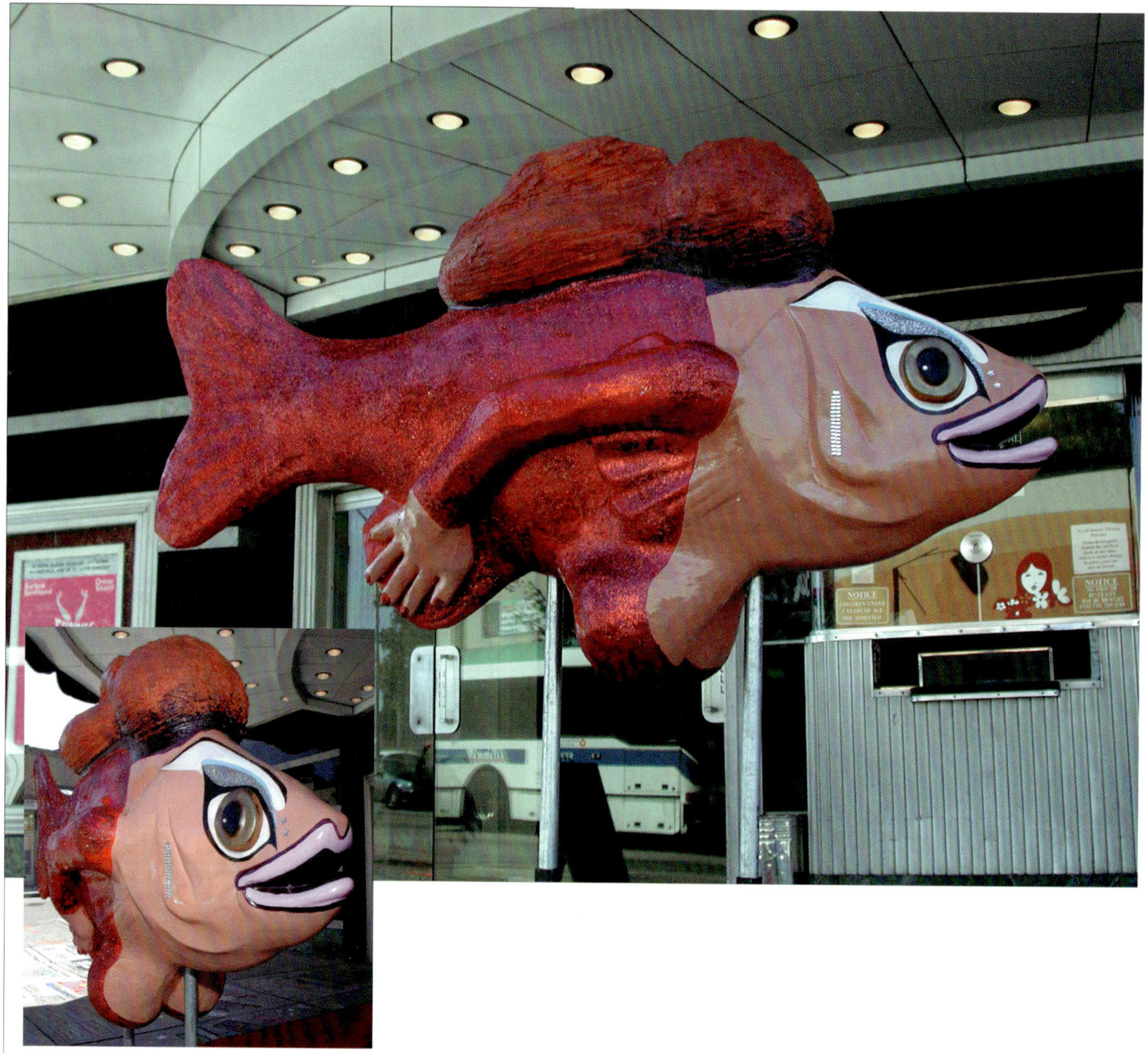

DIVINE FISH OUT OF WATERS

Anthea Zeltzman

Belvedere Improvement Assocation/
The Senator Theatre

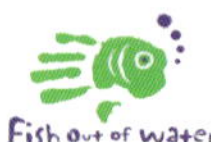

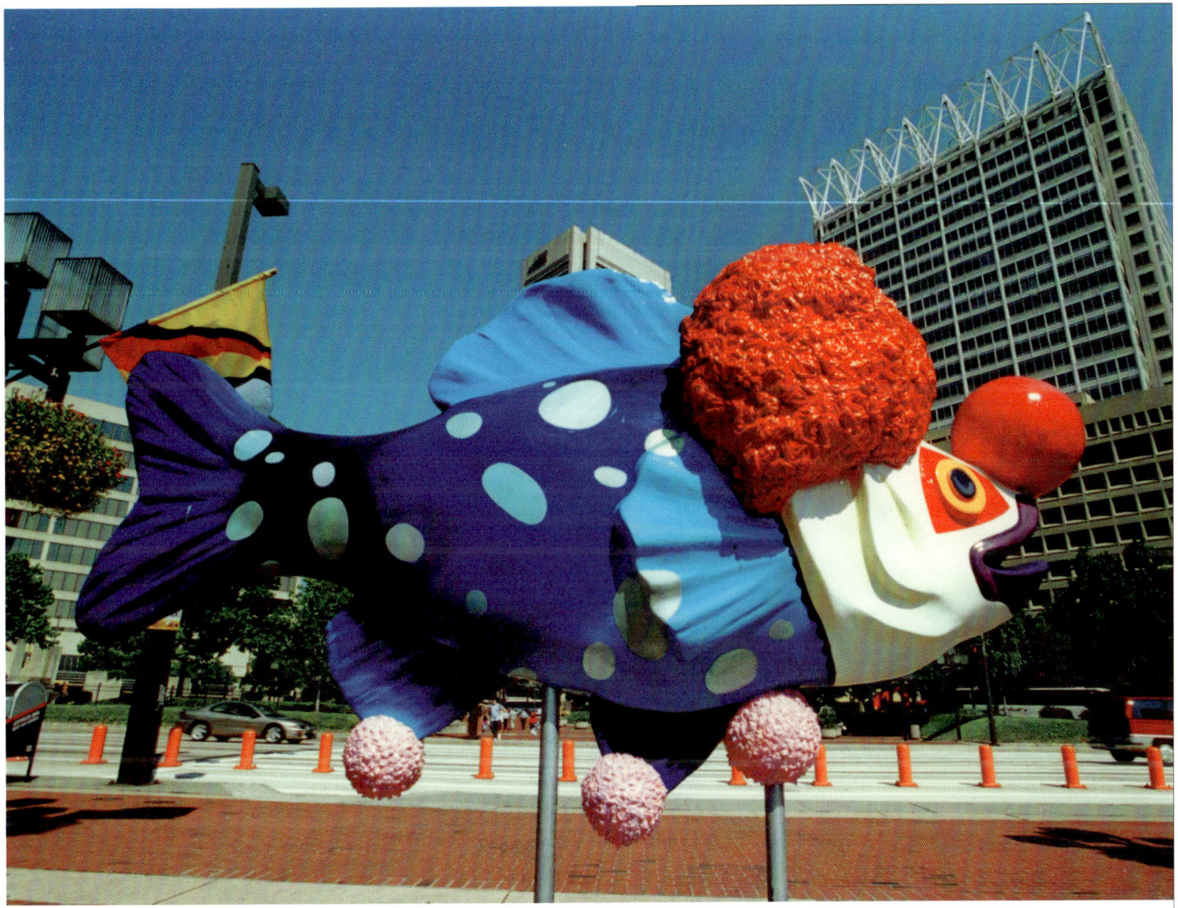

CLOWN FISH
Mike W. Anthony & Sarah Barnes
Chesapeake Partners

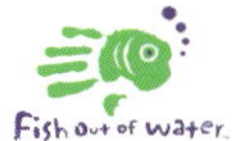

CATFISH
Laurence Hurst
Nathan and
Suzanne Cohen Foundation

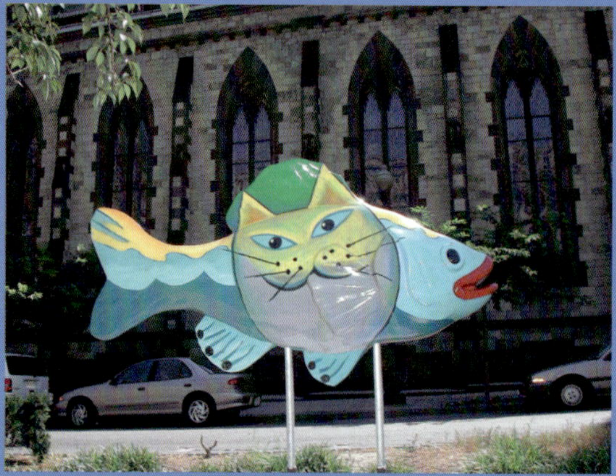

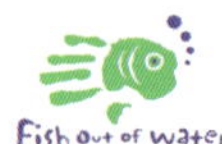

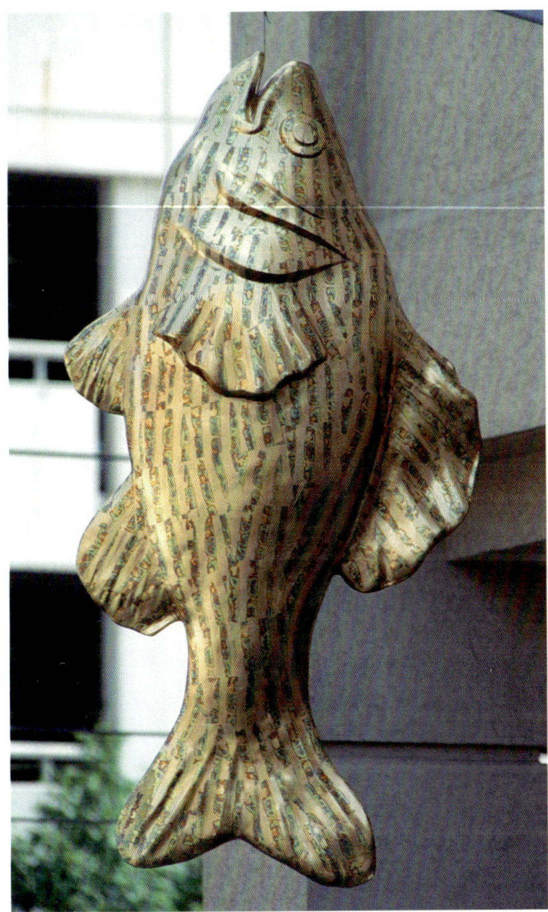

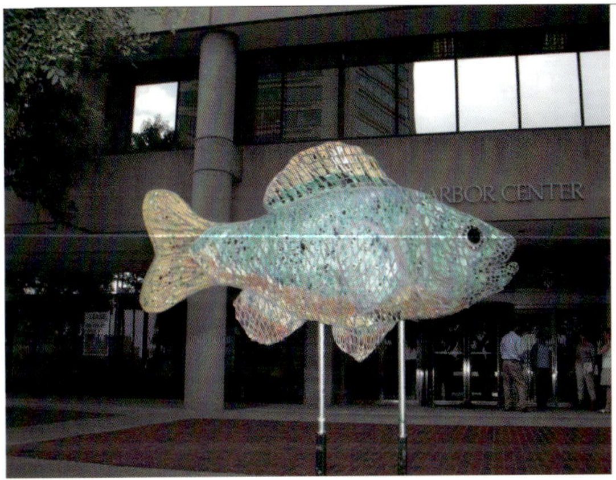

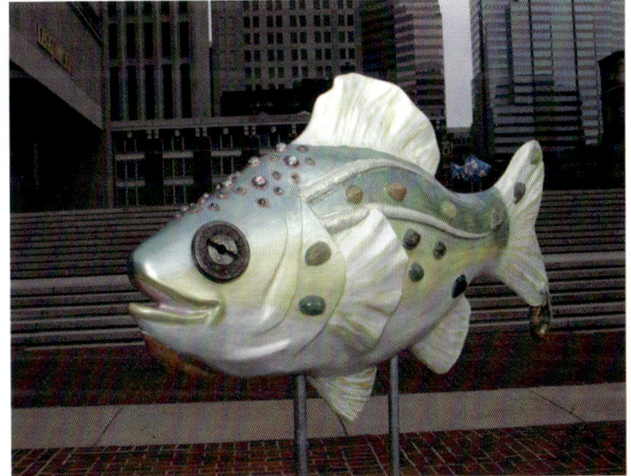

Left:

GOLDYLOX
Dan Van Allen
Holiday Inn

Top right:

MOSAIC/SYSCOD
Ken Hankins
SYSCOM Inc.

Bottom right:

BOHEMIAN BASS
Jerry Romanow
Chesapeake Advertising, Inc.

FISH WITH CHARACTER

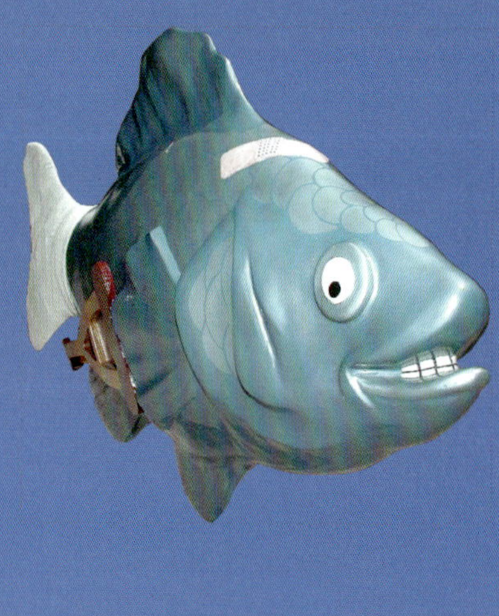

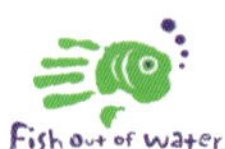

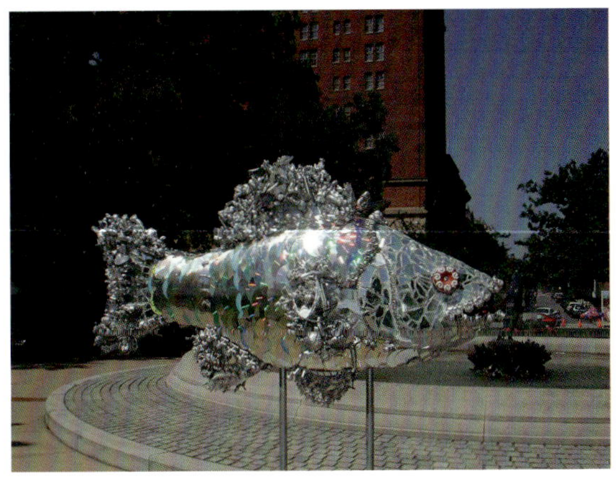

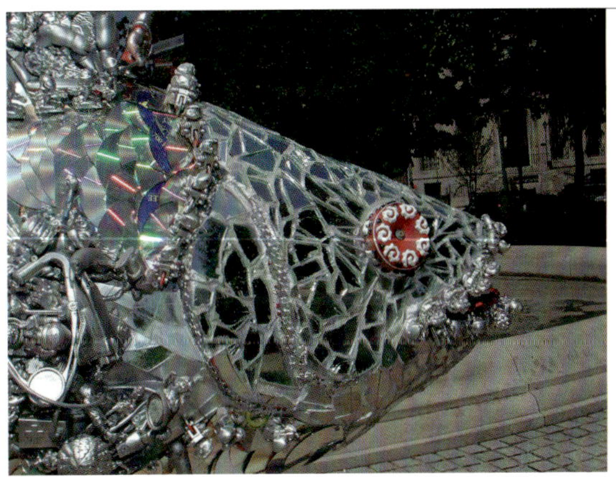

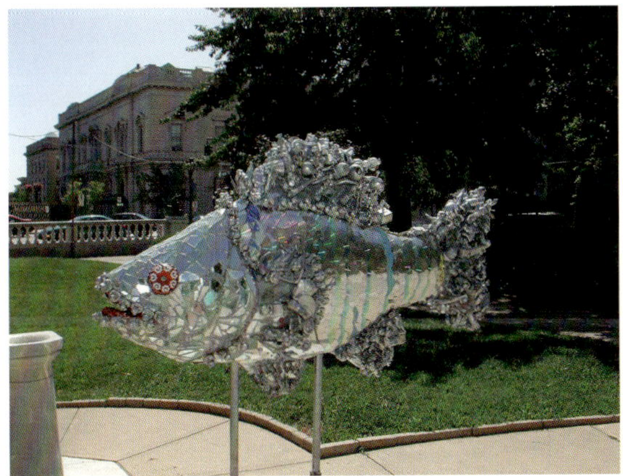

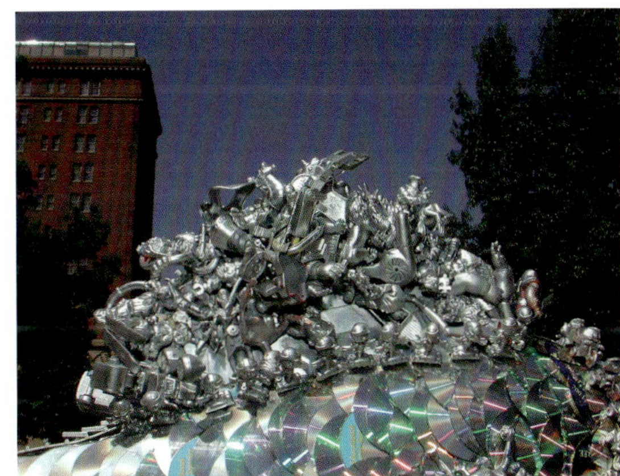

WE

Mary Cate-Carroll

Greater Baltimore Medical Center

CareFirst BlueFish

Steven Hammett

CareFirst BlueCross BlueShield

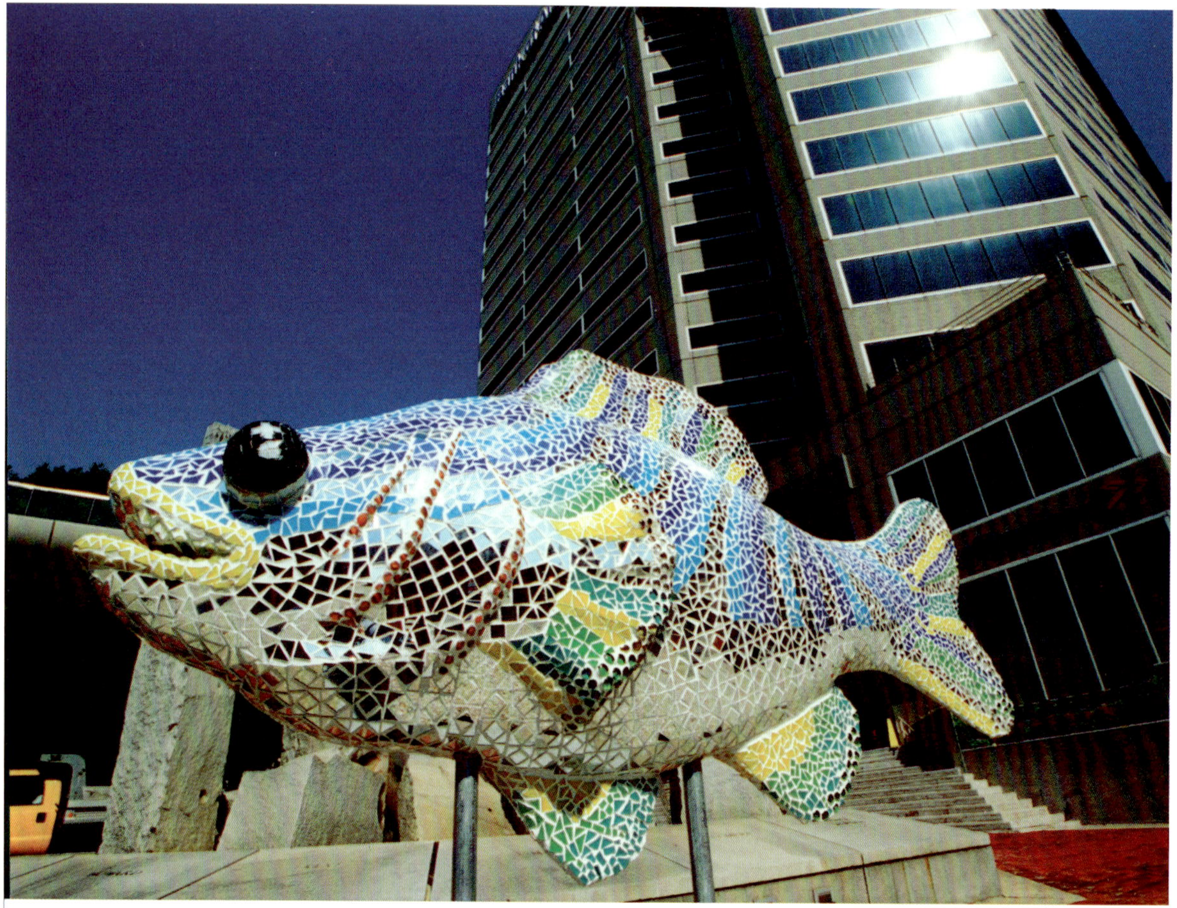

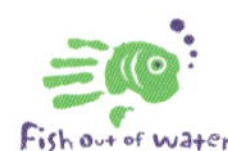

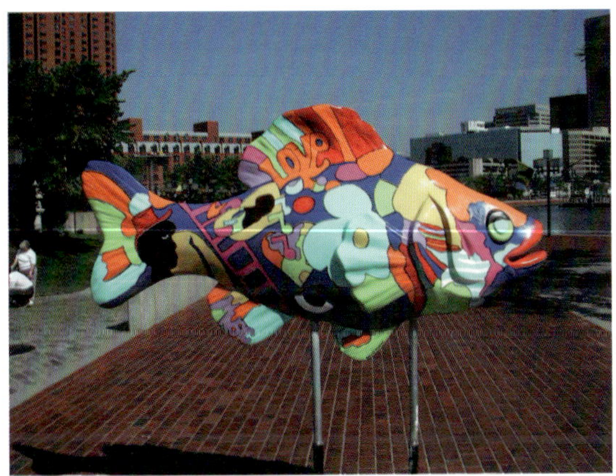

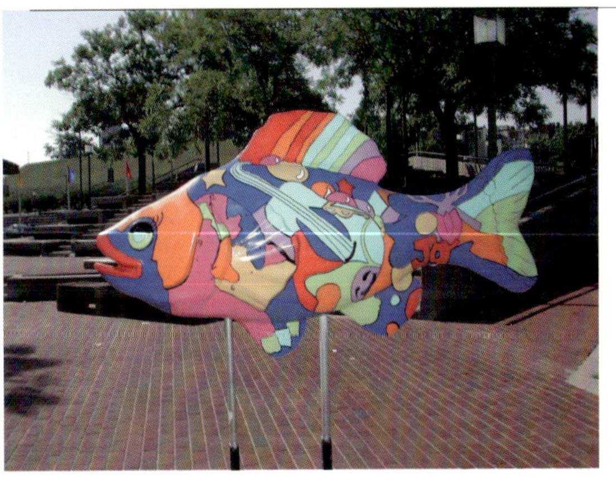

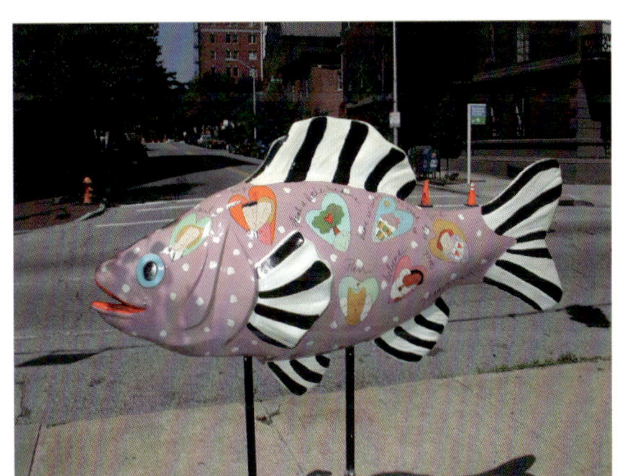

Top left and right:

GOODNESS
Shallie Murphy
Harry and Jeanette Weinberg Foundation

Bottom left:

REFLECT
William Niebauer
Brown Capital Management, Inc.

Bottom right:

HEART FISH
Sandra Magsamen
The Pleasure of Your Company

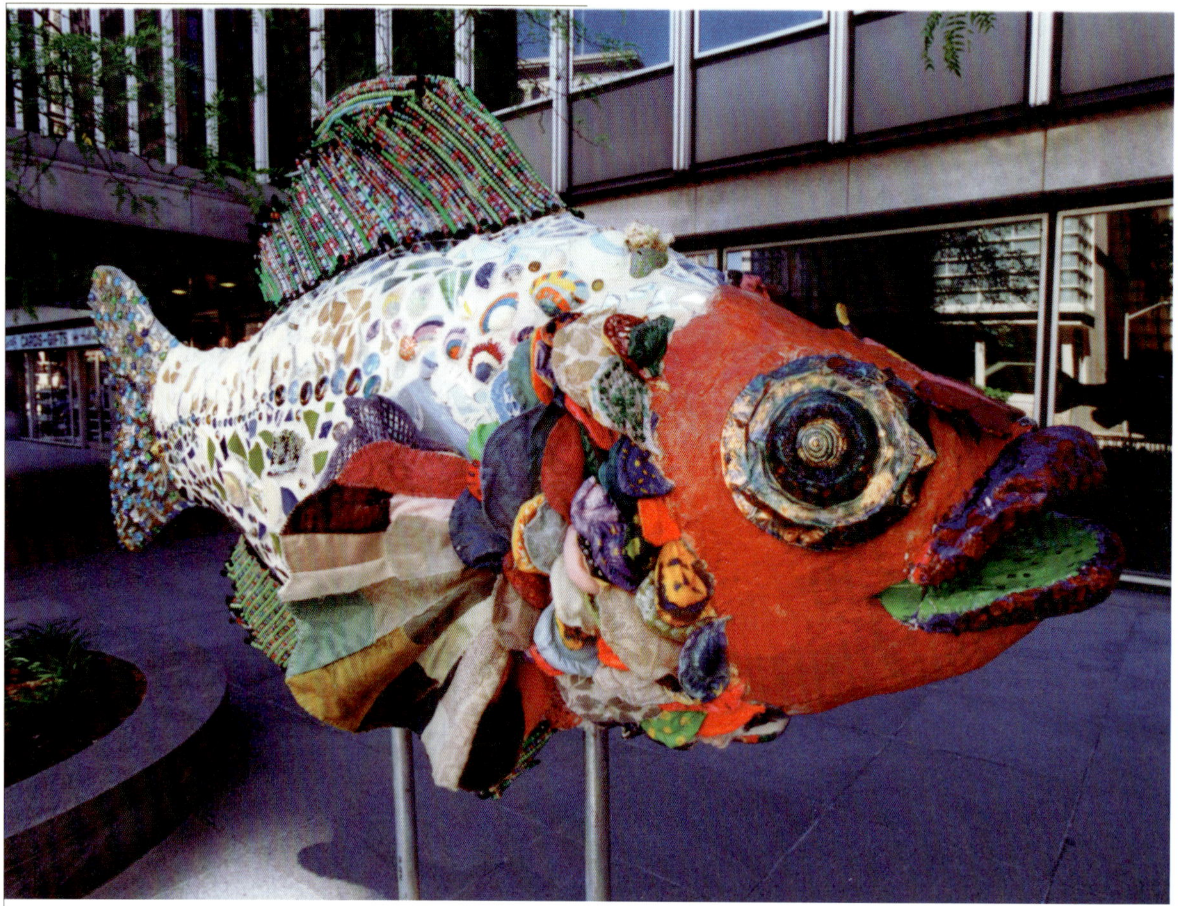

SEA CHANGE

April K. Ballard & Health Care for the Homeless Art Expression Group

Rosemore, Inc.

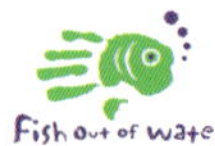

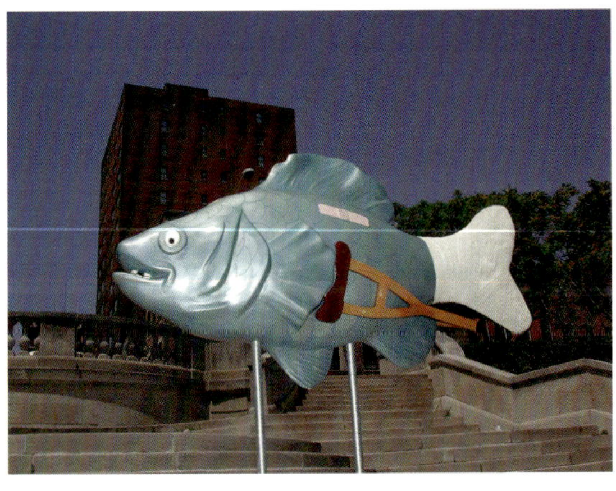

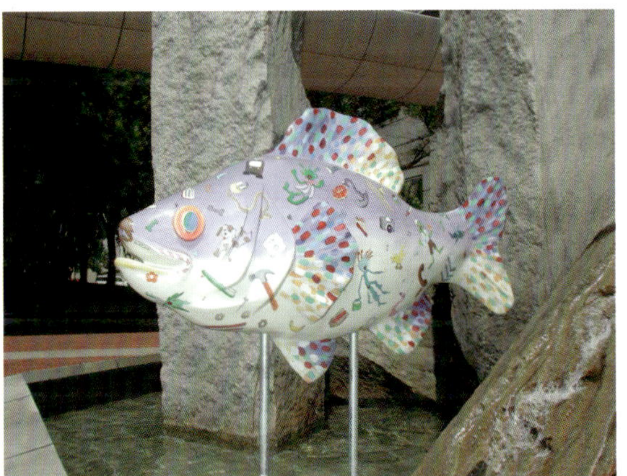

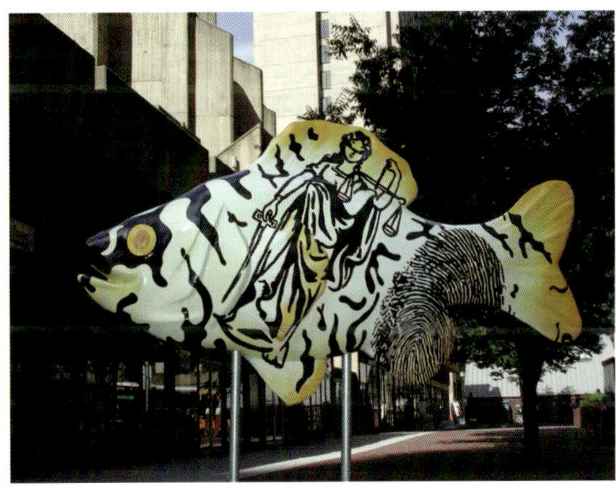

Clockwise, from top left:

CRUTCH OF THE DAY
Anthony Cervino
Mercy Medical Center

SCALES OF JUSTICE
Mike W. Anthony & Sarah Barnes
Adelberg, Rudow, Dorf & Hendler

FISH FAMILY VALUES
Rodney Cook
Bank of America

FISH IN THE WATER

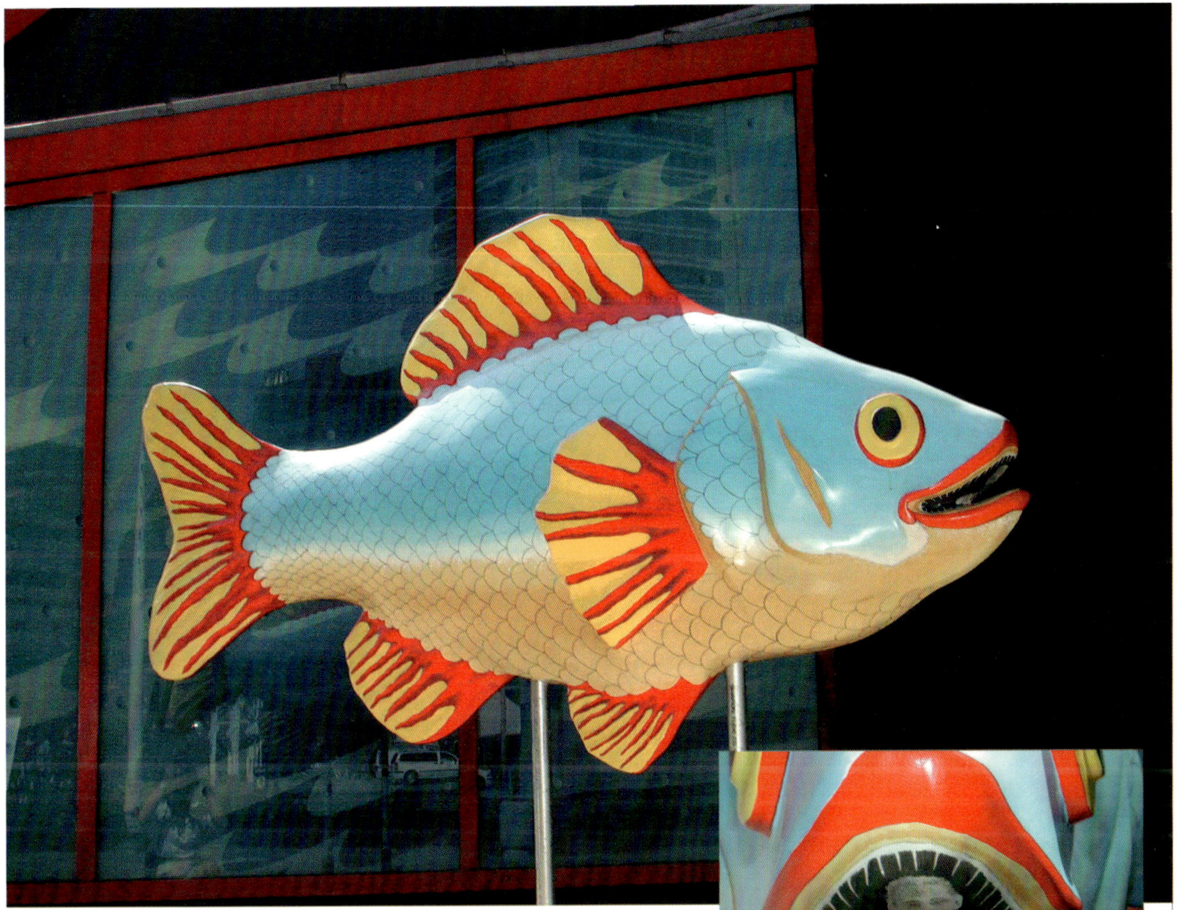

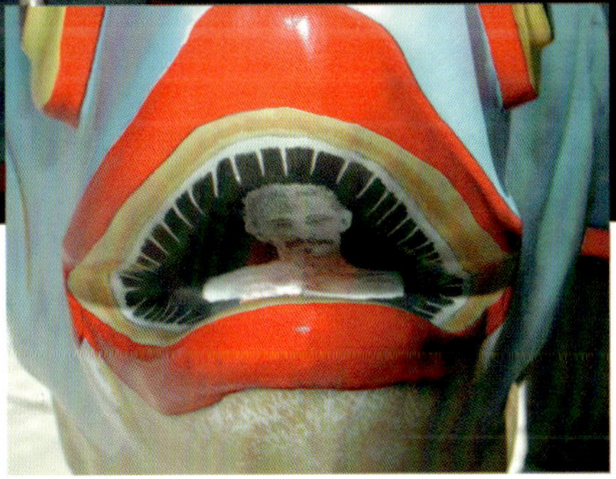

DARBY FISH
Michael Darby
Fish Out of Water

(Inset: Artist self-portrait)

A-LURE OF THE SEA

Anthony Cervino

MetLife Auto & Home

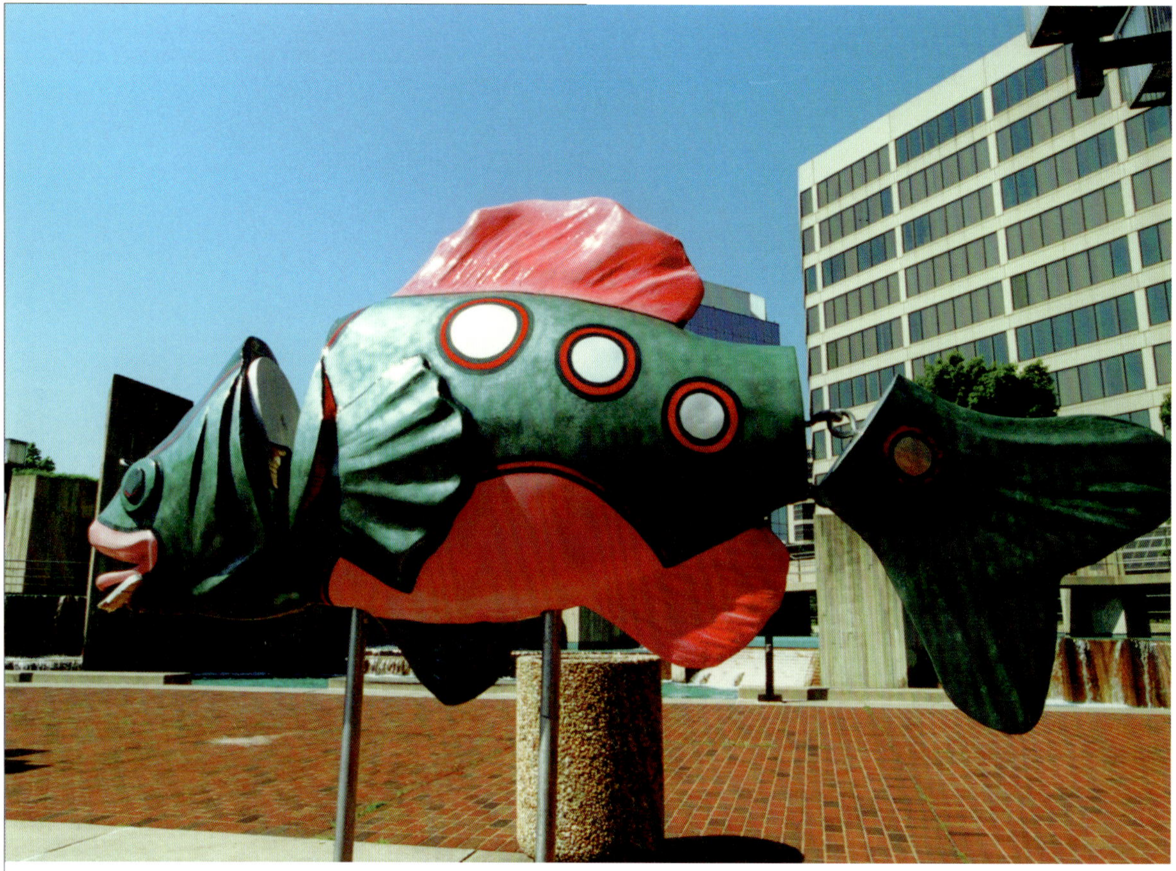

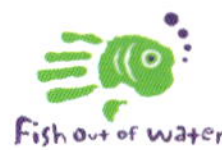

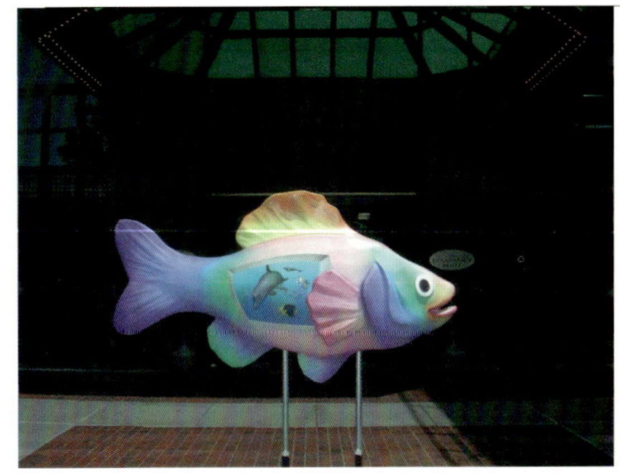

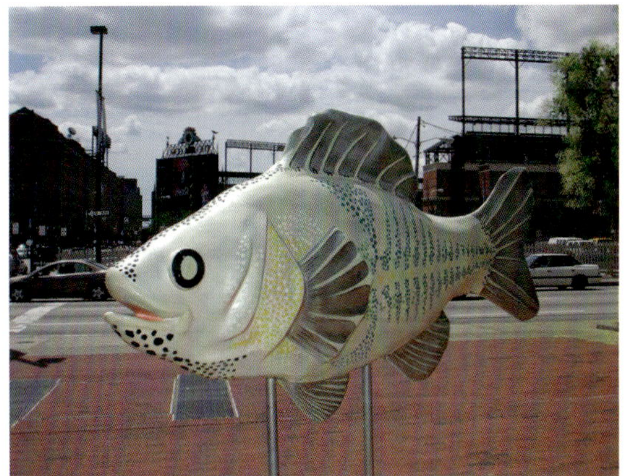

Top:

AQUA LUNG
G. Byron Peck
Renaissance Harborplace Hotel

Bottom:

BARE BONES
Jo Houtz
Marriott Hotels International
Baltimore City

SHARK LARK
Anthony Cervino
National Aquarium in Baltimore

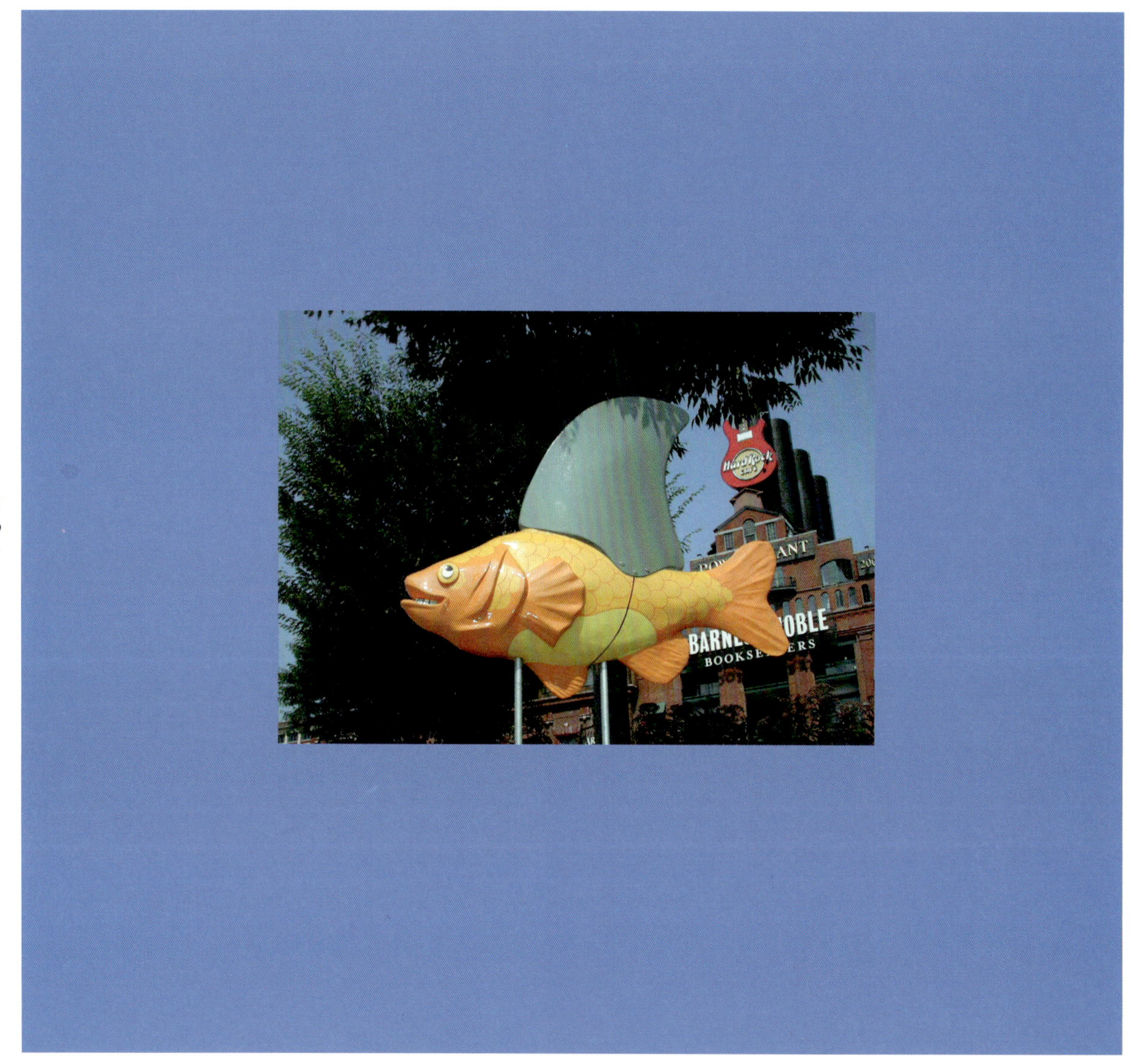

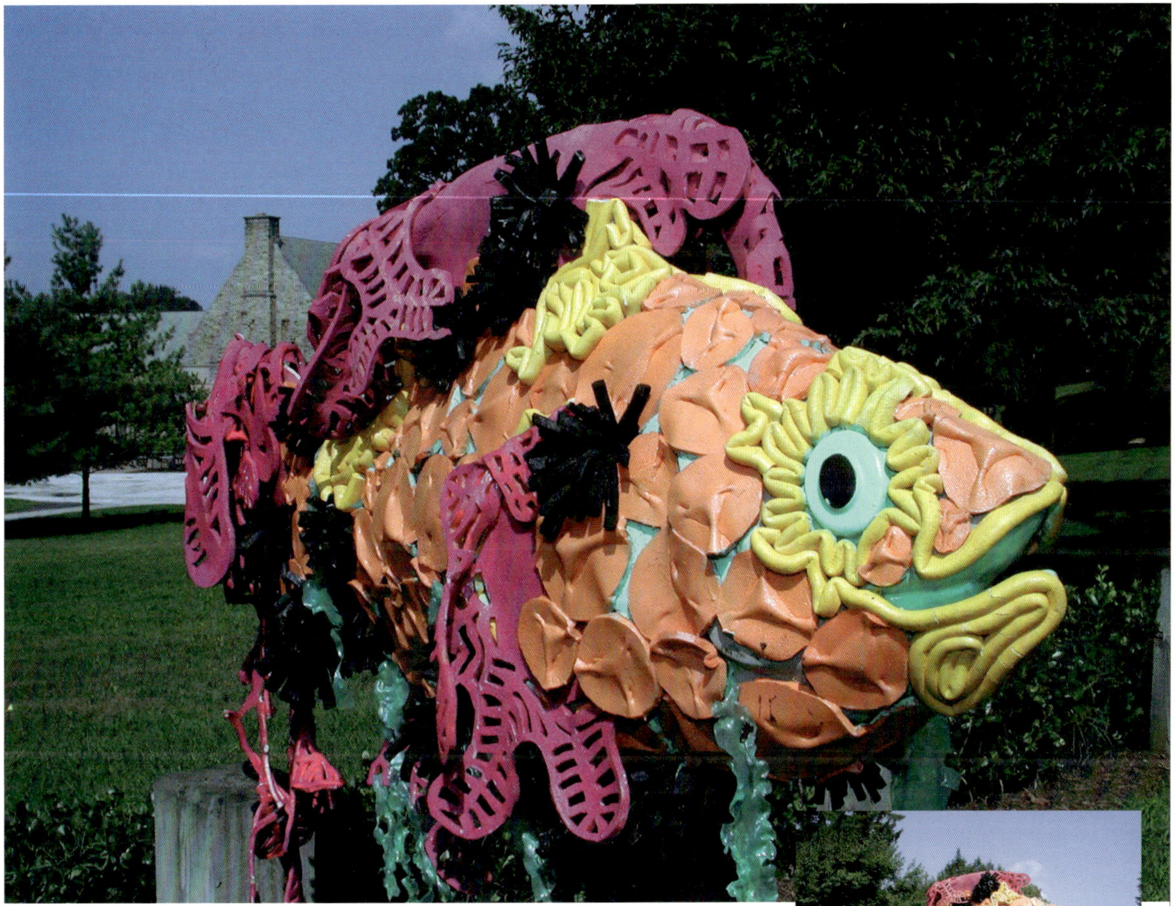

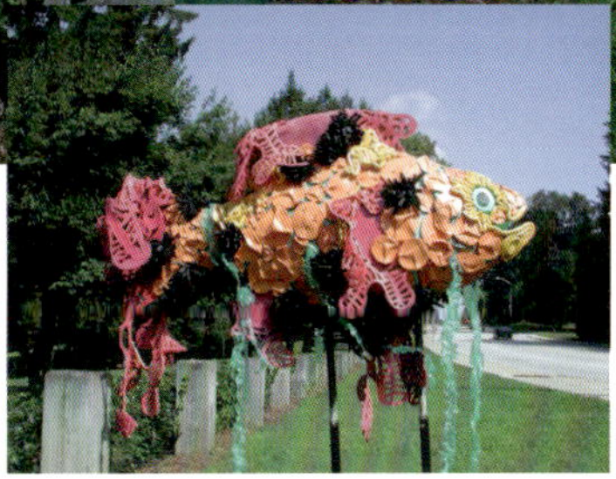

MIGRATORY CORAL REEF

Flora McGarrell

Friends School of Baltimore

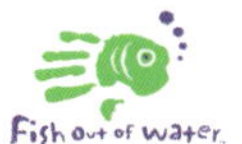

Left to Right:

ANNABELLE THE SEA FLOWER FISH
Laura Sharp Wilson
Fish Out of Water

LIFE AT SEA
Dietrich Maune
Piper Marbury Rudnick & Wolfe LLP

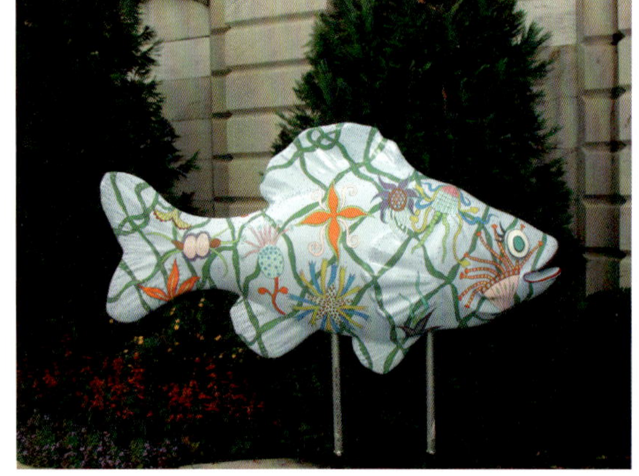

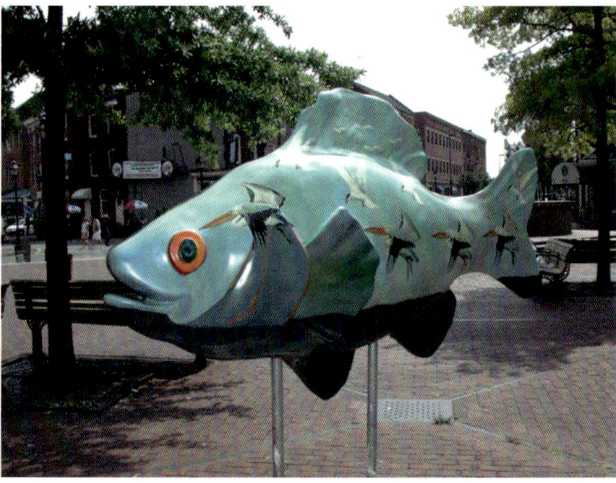

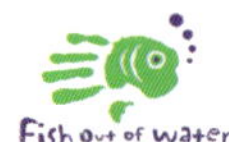

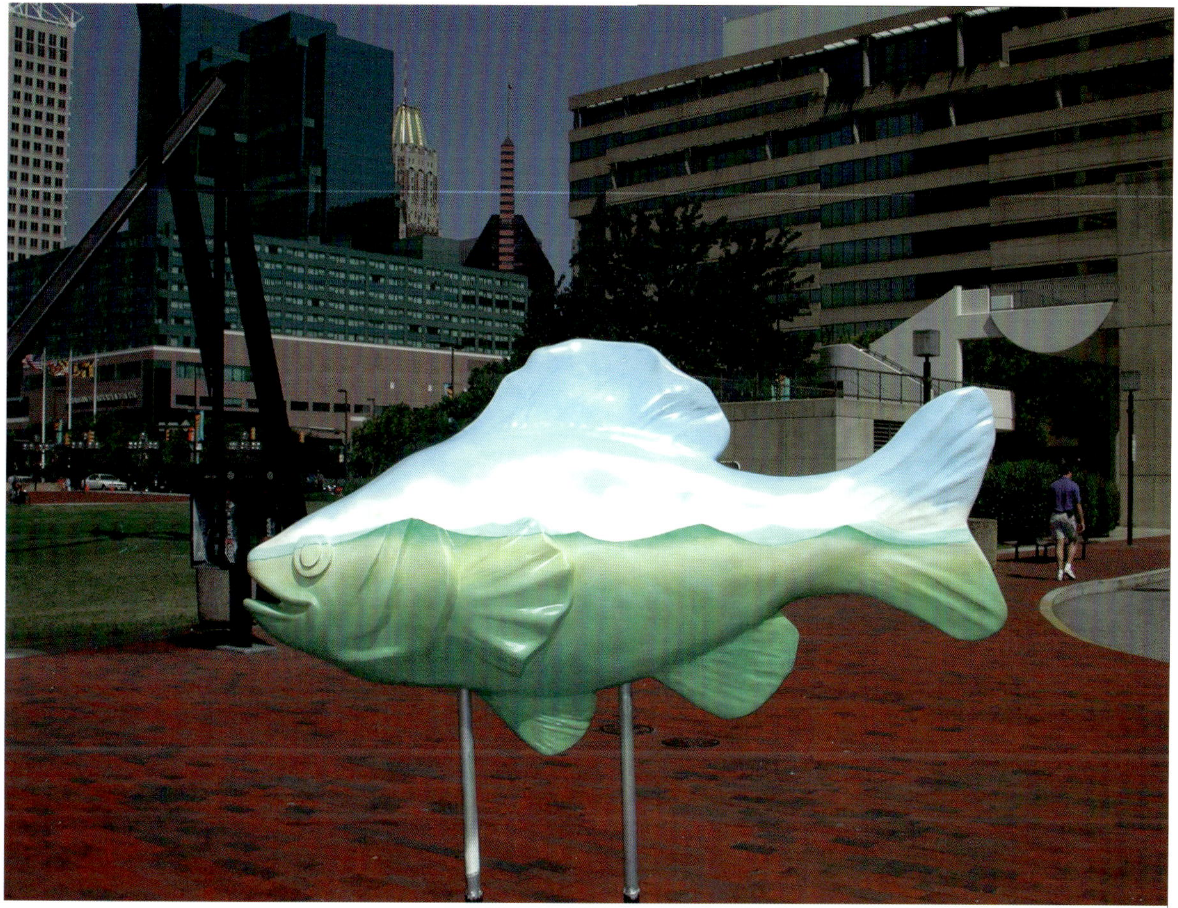

FISH CONTAINING THE SEA
Kevin MacDonald
WBAL TV11 Insta-Weather

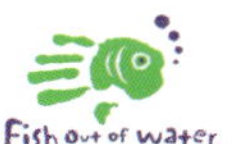

FISH ON THE LOOSE

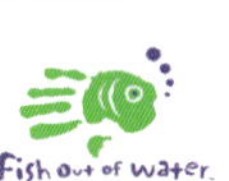

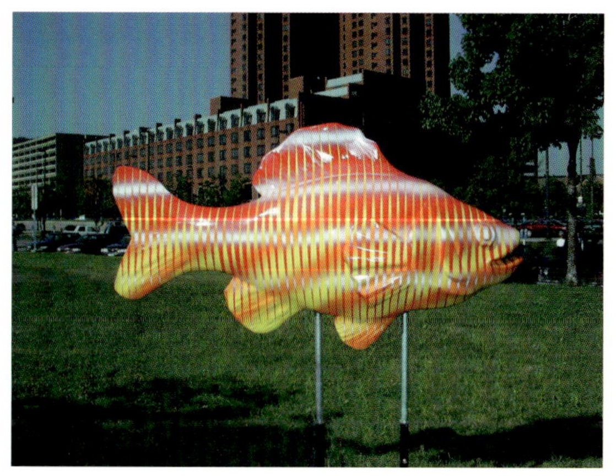

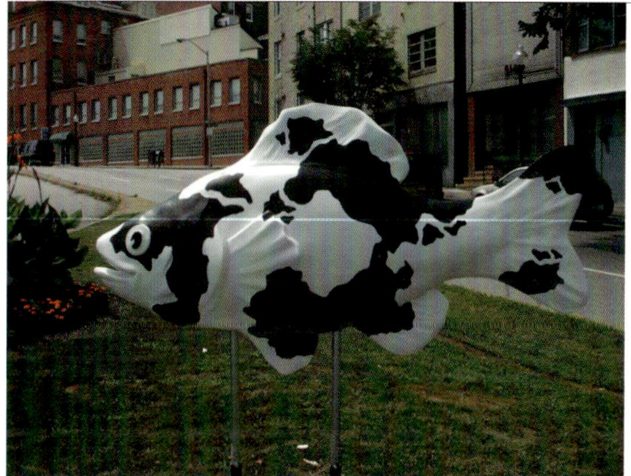

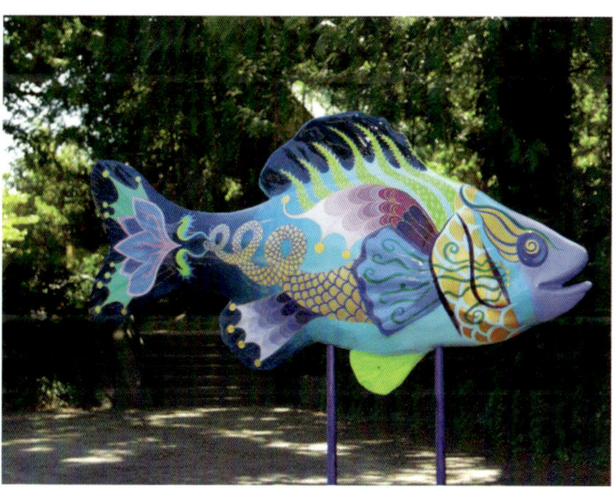

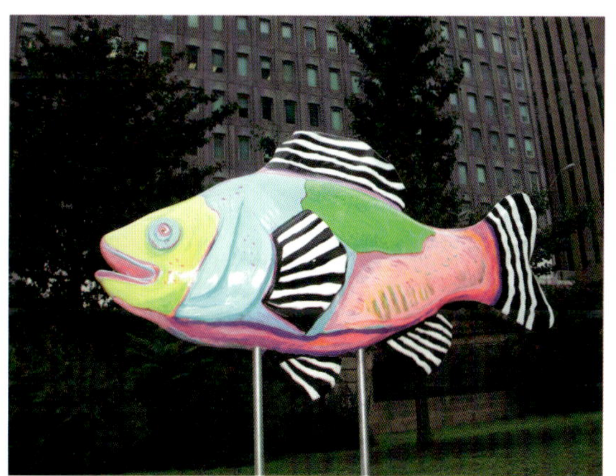

Clockwise, from top left:

HOT FISH
Chul-Hyun Ahn
Trigen Energy Baltimore

HOLSTEIN
Bill Shimek
Fish Out of Water

ZEBRA FISH
Judy Heimann
Fish Out of Water

DRAGON FISH
Gail Gorlitzz
The Columbus Center

PENNY
Jack Scott
KPMG LLP

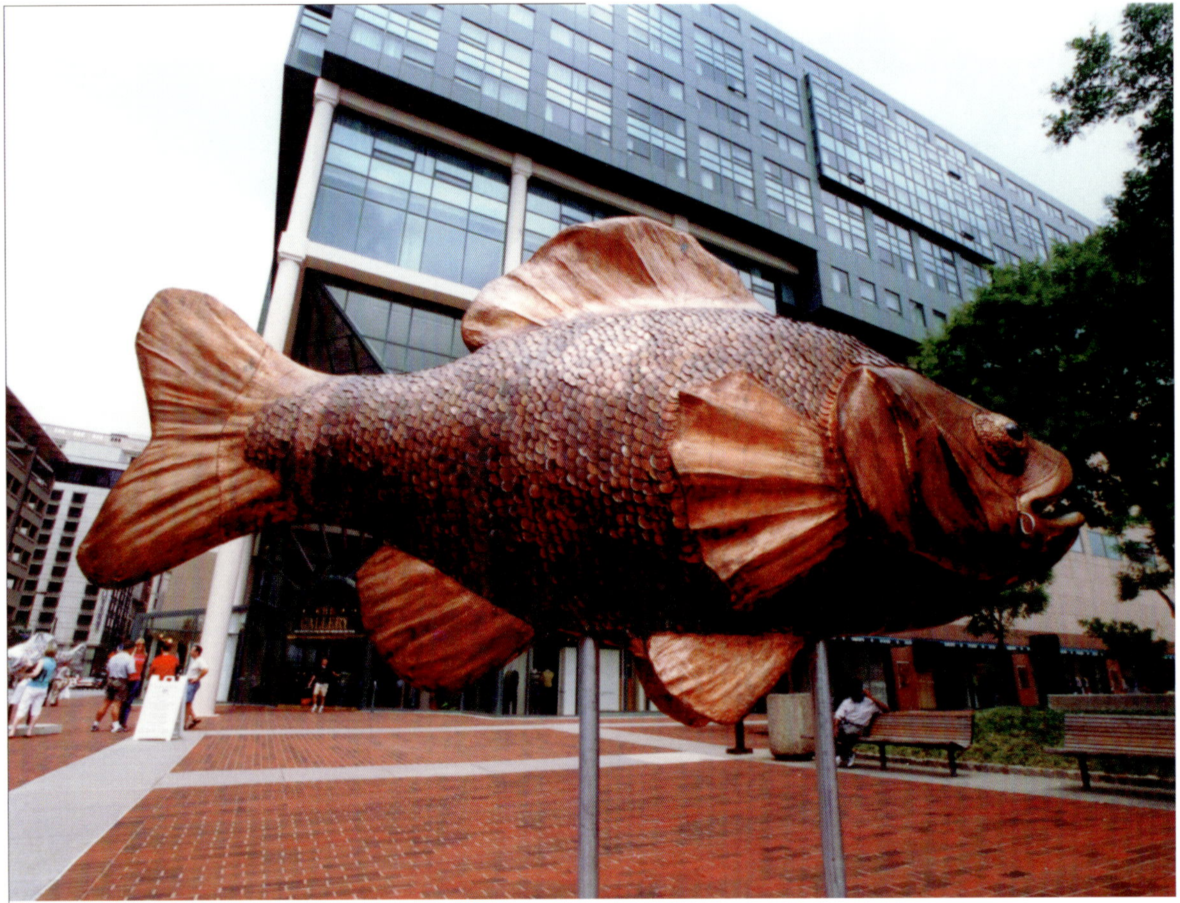

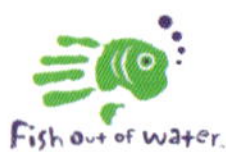

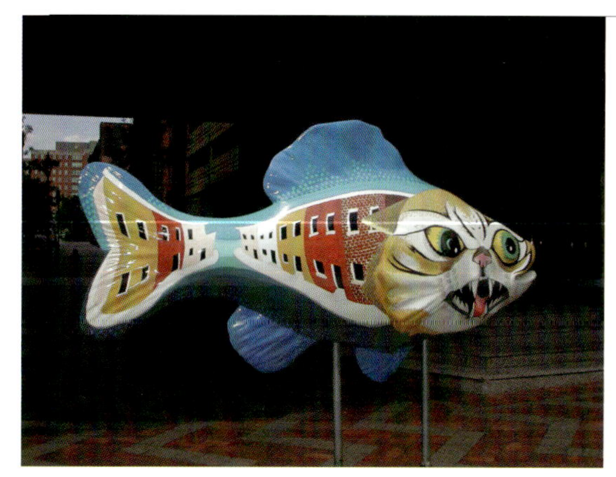

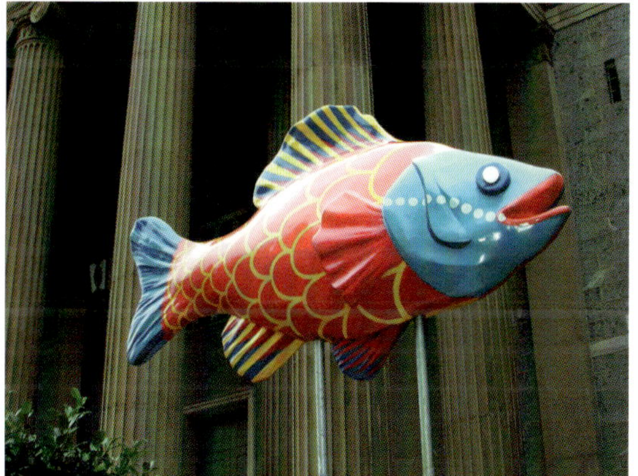

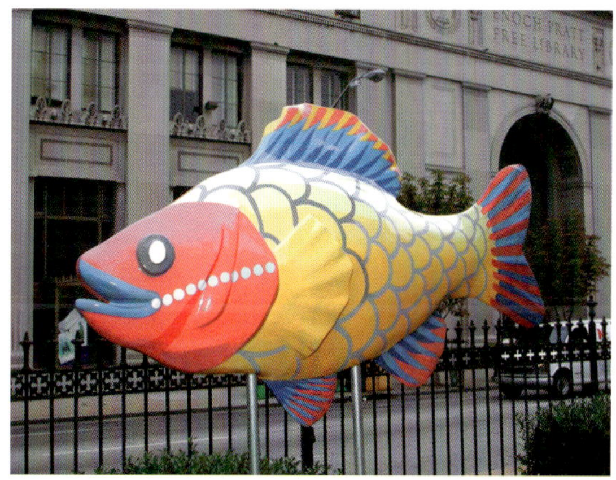

Top:

ALLEY CATFISH
Ronald R. Russell & Laura Vernon-Russell
Otis Warren & Company

Left and Right:

HOLY MACKEREL!
Bennard Perlman
The Basilica of the Assumption

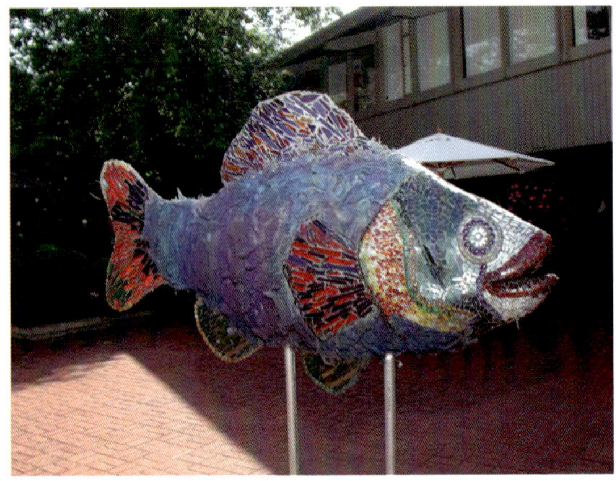

Top right:

RUPERT
Maria-Theresa Fernandes
The Village of Cross Keys

Bottom left and right:

HIGH FIN-ANCE
Craig Brown
Bunting Family Foundation

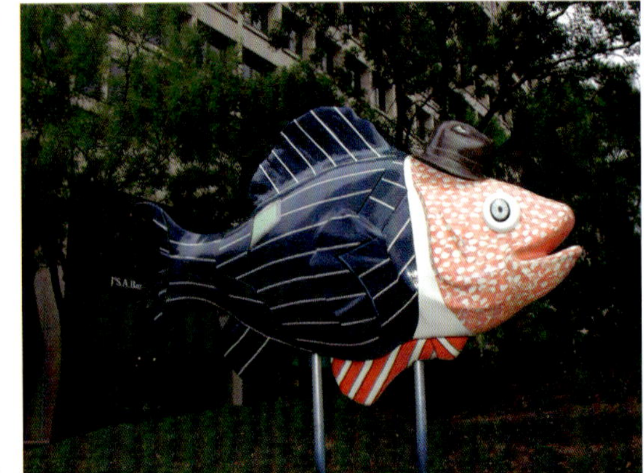

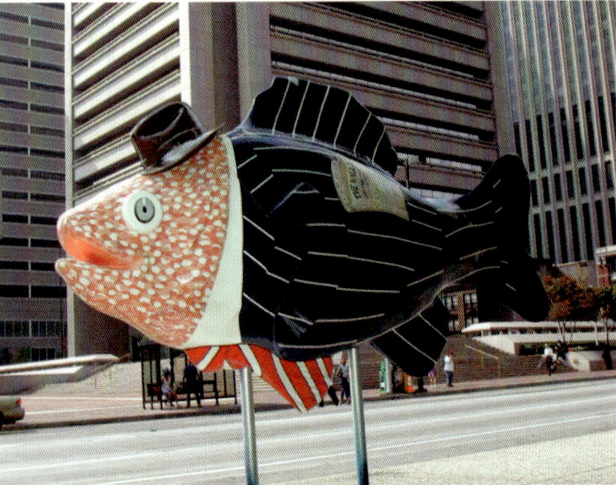

INDEX

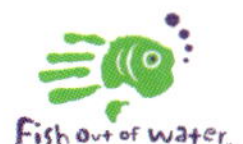

The following fish were still "in the water" at the time we went to press. Therefore, photos of these fish are not in the book, but they are all part of our public art display.

Parrot Fish
Larcia Premo
WMAR

Cobalt Blue
Bill Adler
Fish Out of Water

Sapphire Midnight Garden
Rufus Toomey
Anheiser Busch Companies

Chuck Go Lightly
Randall Gornowich
Anheiser Busch Companies

Remains
Joe Rizza
Anheiser Busch Companies

Belly of the Bay
Peggy Fox,
Anheiser Busch Companies

Fishscape
Joe Giordano
Belair Edison
Neighborhoods, Inc.

Kid Fish
Anne Hynes
Annie E. Casey Foundation
for the children and families
of East Baltimore

Fish Face
Espi Frazier
Fish Out of Water

Zen Fish
Jacquie Shane
Fish Out of Water

Shriver Caught at the Net
Nanette Ferreri
The Chevy Chase Bank Tennis
Challenge Presented by the
Baltimore Sun

Shellfish
Mary Hennessey
Radio One

See What I Sea?
Lee Anna Will
Waverly Main Street Businesses

Smiley Fish
Nina Rutledge
Anheiser Busch Companies

Old Glory
Access Art
Washington Boulevard Main
Street Program

Halibrick
Christina McCleary
Fannie Mae

Baltimore Fish
James Hennessey
Fish Out of Water